Motivated Reinforcement Learning

Kathryn E. Merrick · Mary Lou Maher

Motivated Reinforcement Learning

Curious Characters for Multiuser Games

 Springer

Dr. Kathryn E. Merrick
School of Information Technology
  and Electrical Engineering
University of New South Wales
Australian Defence Force Academy
Building 16
Northcott Drive, Canberra ACT 2600
Australia
k.merrick@adfa.edu.au

Prof. Mary Lou Maher
Faculty of Architecture, Design, and Planning
University of Sydney
148 City Road
Sydney NSW 2006
Australia
mary@arch.usyd.edu.au

ISBN 978-3-540-89186-4   e-ISBN 978-3-540-89187-1
DOI 10.1007/978-3-540-89187-1
Springer Dordrecht Heidelberg London New York

Library of Congress Control Number: 2009926102

ACM Computing Classification (1998): I.2, I.3, H.5, K.8

Cover design: KünkelLopka, Heidelberg

Printed on acid-free paper

Springer is part of Springer Science+Business Media (www.springer.com)

Preface

The past few years have seen steady improvements in computer technology for graphics, sound, networking and processing power. Using these technologies, online virtual worlds like *Second Life*, *There*, and *Active Worlds* are emerging as platforms for multiuser computer games, social interaction, education, design, health, defence and commerce. Computer-controlled, non-player characters facilitate games and activities in these worlds and may interact with hundreds of thousands of human-controlled characters. However, artificial intelligence technology to control non-player characters has, so far, lagged behind advances in other virtual world technologies. There is now a need for more believable and intelligent non-player characters to support and enhance virtual world applications.

This book presents a new artificial intelligence technique – motivated reinforcement learning – for the development of non-player characters in multiuser games. Both theoretical and practical issues are addressed for developing adaptive, dynamic non-player characters. Focus applications include multiuser, role-playing and simulation games.

Humans and animals have the ability to focus and adapt their behaviour. Motivations, such as hunger, curiosity or peer pressure, inspire natural systems to exhibit behaviour that forms distinct cycles, is adaptive and is oriented towards different tasks at different times. These behavioural traits are also an advantage for artificial agents in complex or dynamic environments, where only a small amount of available information may be relevant at a particular time, and relevant information changes over time. Motivated reinforcement learning combines computational models of motivation with advanced machine learning algorithms – to empower non-player characters to self-identify new tasks on which to focus their attention and learn about. The result is an agent model for non-player characters that continuously generate new behaviours as a response to their experiences in their environment. Motivated reinforcement learning can achieve advantages over existing character control algorithms by enabling the development of non-player characters that can generate dynamic behaviour and adapt in time with an unpredictable, changing game environment.

Motivated reinforcement learning transforms the capability of non-player characters because it provides non-player characters with a mechanism for open-ended, online adaptation of their own behaviour. The aim of this book is to provide game programmers, and those with an interest in artificial intelligence, with the knowledge required to develop adaptable, intelligent agents that can take on a life of their own in complex, dynamic environments.

Motivated learning is an exciting, emerging research topic in the field of artificial intelligence. The development of motivated machines is at the cutting edge of artificial intelligence and cognitive modelling research and contributes to the development of machines that are able to learn new skills and achieve goals that were not predefined by human engineers. This opens the way both for new types of artificial agents, and new types of computer games. This book provides an in-depth look at new algorithms for motivated reinforcement learning and offers insights into the strengths, limitations and future development of motivated agents for gaming applications.

Part I – Non-Player Characters and Reinforcement Learning

Chapter 1 – Non-Player Characters in Multiuser Games
Chapter 2 – Motivation in Natural and Artificial Agents
Chapter 3 – Towards Motivated Reinforcement Learning
Chapter 4 – Comparing the Behaviour of Learning Agents

The first part of this book synthesises the basic concepts of non-player characters, motivation, and reinforcement learning. To highlight the need for new kinds of intelligent agents for computer games, Chap. 1 examines current multiuser games, the roles of non-player characters and existing approaches to artificial intelligence used in games. As inspiration for the development of motivated agent models, Chap. 2 examines theories of motivation proposed by psychologists and models of motivation used in artificial agents. Chapter 3 introduces the computational theory and notation for reinforcement learning and the ways in which computational models of motivation fit within this framework. Chapter 4 examines how the behaviour of learning agents and non-player characters can be compared and evaluated.

Part II – Developing Curious Characters Using Motivated Reinforcement Learning

Chapter 5 – Curiosity, Motivation and Attention Focus
Chapter 6 – Motivated Reinforcement Learning Agents

Part II of this book presents a framework for the development of non-player characters as motivated reinforcement learning agents. Chapter 5 presents models of motivation for this framework, while Chap. 6 describes how these models can be incorporated with different reinforcement learning algorithms.

In Chap. 5, motivation is modelled as a process that starts with observations and events as potential learning tasks, selects tasks to learn, applies psychologically inspired, experience-based reward signals, and then arbitrates over reward signals for different tasks to compute a motivation signal. The motivation signal directs the reinforcement learning algorithm as a replacement for a task-specific reward signal. This chapter concludes by describing two models of curiosity using interest and competence to compute a motivation signal for non-player characters.

In Chap. 6, three motivated reinforcement learning algorithms are presented that combine the two computational models of motivation with flat reinforcement learning, multioption reinforcement learning and hierarchical reinforcement learning. These algorithms enable non-player characters to learn behaviours with different levels of recall and ability to reuse learned behaviours.

Part III – Curious Characters in Games

Chapter 7 – Curious Characters for Multiuser Games
Chapter 8 – Curious Characters for Games in Complex, Dynamic
*   Environments*
Chapter 9 – Curious Characters for Games in Second Life

In Part III, the theory from previous chapters is applied in a range of practical game scenarios. Chapter 7 demonstrates six different types of curious characters in small-scale, isolated game scenarios. Case studies and empirical results are examined to provide insight into the type of behaviour achieved by characters using motivated reinforcement learning. Chapter 8 moves curious characters into three more complex, dynamic environments and examines the changes in their behaviour.

Chapter 9 presents a demonstration of motivated reinforcement learning for controlling characters in a simulation game, in which player characters can make open-ended modifications to the game world while the game is in progress. This case study provides an evaluation of the adaptive, multitask learning performance of motivated reinforcement learning with respect to a specific application. The game is implemented in the *Second Life* virtual environment. This case study shows how a single agent model can be used to develop different characters by exploiting the ability of motivated reinforcement learning agents to develop different behaviours based on their experiences in their environment.

Part IV – Future

Chapter 10 – Towards the Future

In Chap. 10, the strengths and limitations of motivated reinforcement learning are considered and used as a basis for discussion of the future directions for motivated agents and multiuser computer games. Advances in computational models of motivation, motivated learning models and their application to multiuser games are considered.

University of New South Wales, February 2009   Kathryn Merrick
University of Sydney, February 2009   Mary Lou Maher

Acronyms

CFG	Context-Free Grammar
DDA	Dynamic Difficulty Adjustment
GPI	Generalised Policy Interaction
HRL	Hierarchical Reinforcement Learning
HSOM	Habituated Self-Organising Map
MDP	Markov Decision Process
MFRL	Motivated Flat Reinforcement Learning
MHRL	Motivated Hierarchical Reinforcement Learning
MMORL	Motivated Multioption Reinforcement Learning
MMORPG	Massively Multiplayer Online Role-Playing Game
MRL	Motivated Reinforcement Learning
MSL	Motivated Supervised Learning
MUL	Motivated Unsupervised Learning
NPC	Non-Player Character
PCG	Procedural Content Generation
POMDP	Partially Observable Markov Decision Process
RL	Reinforcement Learning
RPG	Role-Playing Game
SL	Supervised Learning
SMDP	Semi-Markov Decision Process
SOM	Self-Organising Map
TD	Temporal Difference
UL	Unsupervised Learning

Contents

Part I
Non-Player Characters and Reinforcement Learning

Chapter 1
Non-Player Characters in Multiuser Games

Massively multiuser, persistent, online virtual worlds are emerging as important platforms for multiuser computer games, social interaction, education, design, defence and commerce. In these virtual worlds, non-player characters use artificial intelligence to take on roles as storytellers, enemies, opponents, partners and facilitators. Non-player characters share their world with hundreds of thousands of creative, unpredictable, human controlled characters. As the complexity and functionality of multiuser virtual worlds increases, non-player characters are becoming an increasingly challenging application for artificial intelligence techniques [1]. The rise of multiuser games in particular has created a need for new kinds of artificial intelligence approaches that can produce characters with adaptive and complex behaviours for large-scale, dynamic game environments. Players are demanding more believable and intelligent non-player characters to enhance their gaming experience [2].

Motivated reinforcement learning is an emerging artificial intelligence technology that provides a theoretical and practical approach for developing adaptive characters for multiuser games. Motivated reinforcement learning has advantages over existing character control algorithms because it allows the development of non-player characters that can generate dynamic behaviour and adapt in time with an unpredictable, changing game environment. Motivated reinforcement learning uses computational models of human motivation – such as curiosity, interest and competence – to empower non-player characters to self-identify new tasks on which to focus their attention. The characters then use a reinforcement learning component to learn behavioural cycles to perform these tasks. The result is an agent model for non-player characters that are continually evolving new behaviours as a response to their experiences in their environment.

Motivated reinforcement learning transforms character design because it provides non-player characters with a mechanism for open-ended, online

K.E. Merrick, M.L. Maher, *Motivated Reinforcement Learning*, DOI 10.1007/978-3-540-89187-1_1, adaptation of their own behaviour. In this book we aim to provide game programmers, and those with an interest in artificial intelligence, with the knowledge required to develop adaptable, intelligent non-player characters that can take on a life of their own in dynamic, multiuser virtual worlds.

1.1 Types of Multiuser Games

Computer games can be classified in a range of genres including action games, role-playing games, adventure games, strategy games, simulation games, sports games and racing games. Of these genres, action, role-playing, simulation and racing games have been starting points for multiuser games. A smaller subset again, including role-playing games and simulation games, has emerged as genres for games in persistent virtual worlds. The following sections introduce some distinguishing characteristics of these genres.

1.1.1 Massively Multiplayer Online Role-Playing Games

Massively multiplayer online role-playing games (MMORPGs) such as *World of Warcraft, Ultima Online, Everquest* and *Asheron's Call* are defined by a cast of non-player characters (NPCs) who act as enemies, partners and support characters to provide challenges, offer assistance and support the storyline. These characters exist in a persistent virtual world in which thousands of human players take on roles such as warriors, magicians and thieves and play and interact with NPCs and each other. Over time, the landscape of these worlds evolves and changes as players build their own houses or castles and craft items such as furniture, armour or weapons to personalise their dwellings or sell to other players. Unlike computer games played in non-persistent worlds, persistent game worlds offer months rather than hours of game play, which must be supported by NPCs. However, current technologies used to build non-player enemy, partner and support characters tend to constrain them to a set of fixed behaviours that cannot evolve in time with the world in which they dwell. The resulting behaviour of NPCs has been limited to looping animations with a few scripted action sequences triggered by a player's actions [3].

Sophisticated NPCs have the potential to enrich game worlds by providing opportunities for interesting interactions with players, making the game world more interactive and thus improving the believability of the game [4].

1.1.2 Multiuser Simulation Games

Simulation games such as *The Sims* are distinguished by characters that can respond to certain changes in their environment with new behaviours. Human players modify the circumstances that surround NPCs in order to influence the emergence of certain types of character behaviour for which points may be awarded or which trigger a new phase of the game. Existing simulation and organic simulation games are, however, limited by the set of changes that players may make to the game environment while the game is in progress.

In contrast, human users in current virtual worlds such as *Second Life* [5], *Active Worlds* [6] and *There* [7] can use open-ended modelling tools to create and modify world content. This sort of open-ended modelling is not available in many existing game worlds. The popularity and rapid growth in the user base of open-ended virtual worlds suggests the viability of a new generation of computer game situated in open-ended environments. A key challenge to be overcome in the development of such games, however, is the development of NPCs that can respond autonomously to the open-ended changes to their environment.

1.1.3 Open-Ended Virtual Worlds

The earliest open-ended virtual worlds were text-based, object-oriented, multiuser dungeons (MOOs).[1] MOOs are persistent, multiuser, interactive systems that can be thought of as low-bandwidth virtual worlds. MOOs such as *LambdaMOO* [8] are distinguished from multiuser dungeons (MUDs) by the ability for users to perform object-oriented programming within the MOO server, expanding and changing how the MOO server behaves to all users. Examples of such changes include authoring new rooms and objects, and changing the way the MOO interface operates. These changes are made using a MOO programming language that often features libraries of verbs that can be used by programmers in their coding.

More recently, the improvement in computer graphics technology has made large-scale, 3D virtual worlds possible. Screen shots from *Second Life* and *Active Worlds*, including their 3D modelling tools, are shown in Fig. 1.1 and Fig. 1.2. In these worlds, the virtual landscape can be extended using a combination of primitive shapes and textures to create new buildings, plants, animals and other artefacts. These artefacts can also be assigned dynamic behaviours using in-world scripting tools. The ability to define object

---

[1] MOO = MUD, Object-Oriented.

Fig. 1.1 In the *Second Life* virtual world, complex designs can be created using a combination of primitives, uploaded textures and scripts. Image from [9].

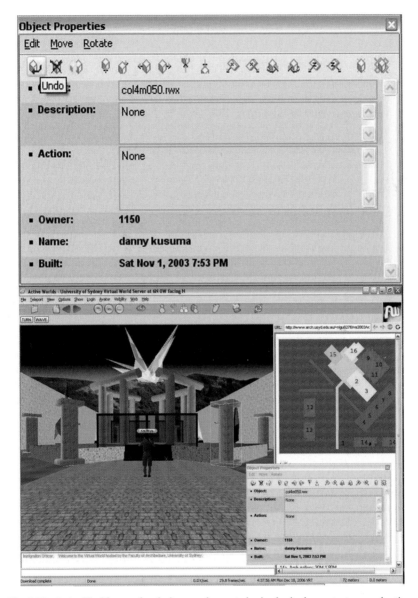

Fig. 1.2 In *Active Worlds*, complex designs can be created using basic shapes, textures and actions. Image from [9].

geometry and assign natural language labels, descriptions and behaviours to designed objects are key aspects that distinguish these virtual worlds as open-ended environments.

While the users of MOOs and 3D virtual worlds have used their open-ended expansion capacities to develop games within these environments, these games have tended to adhere to existing genres such as adventure and role-playing games. The development of games that incorporate NPCs that can respond to the open-ended building capabilities of virtual worlds has been difficult due to the lack of artificial intelligence techniques that can operate in such environments.

1.2 Character Roles in Multiuser Games

NPCs fall into three main categories: enemies, partners and support characters [3]. Enemies are characters that oppose human players in a pseudo-physical sense by attacking the virtual life force of the human player with weapons or magic. Enemies and competitors form a critical character group in a wide range of game genres from action games to strategy or sport games. As a result, the artificial intelligence techniques for enemies and competitors have been a focus of game development.

Partner characters may perform a number of roles within a game. From a competitive perspective, partners take the opposite role to enemies and attempt to protect human players with whom they are allied. Alternatively, however, partner characters might perform non-combat roles to support their human ally. Vendor characters in *Ultima Online*, for example, sell goods on behalf of their human ally. In some games, partner characters may also be taught to perform certain behaviours by players. As with enemy characters, the combat role of partner characters has been well developed. Similarly, existing learning algorithms such as neural networks and reinforcement learning have been used successfully to achieve partner characters that learn from human supervision. The development of characters in a supporting role, however, has so far received less attention.

Support characters are the merchants, tradesmen, guards, innkeepers and so on who support the storyline of the game by offering quests, advice, goods for sale or training. Support characters expand the requirements of artificial intelligence in games beyond those of tactical enemies to social dialogue and behaviours. However, in contrast to enemies or competitors, support characters are among the least sophisticated artificially intelligent characters in current computer games, limited in both their interactions with players and in their behaviour [3]. Conversations with players tend to take the form of scripted speeches interspersed with decision points at which players can affect the direction of the conversation. The behaviour of support characters is generally limited to a looping animation with a few scripted action sequences triggered by a player's exploits. As a result, support characters tend to stand in one place, continually chopping wood or drinking from their mug of ale, until a player initiates an interaction. During the scripted interaction the support character may gesture or move a short distance. However once the interaction is over the character returns to its looping behaviour. The following sections describe the existing artificial intelligence approaches that achieve this behaviour in further detail and highlight the need for new, more adaptive, character control algorithms.

1.3   Existing Artificial Intelligence Techniques for Non-Player Characters in Multiuser Games

Existing technologies used to create NPCs in MMORPGs fall into two broad categories: reflexive agents and learning agents. Reflexive approaches, such as state machines and rule based algorithms, have been common in enemy and support characters while learning algorithms have been used in partners and some enemy characters.

1.3.1   Reflexive Agents

Reflexive behaviour [10] is a preprogrammed response to the state of the environment – a reflex without reasoning. Only recognised states will produce a response. NPCs such as enemies, partners and support characters commonly use reflexive techniques such as state machines, fuzzy logic and rule-based approaches to define their behaviour.

Rule-Based Approaches

Rule-based approaches define a set of rules about states of the game world of the form: `if <condition> then <action>`. If the NPC observes a state that fulfils the `<condition>` of a rule, then the corresponding `<action>` is taken. Only states of the world that meet a `<condition>` will produce an `<action>` response. An example rule from a warrior NPC in the *Baldur's Gate* role-playing game (RPG) [11] is shown in Fig. 1.3. The condition component of this rule is an example of how such rules are domain-dependent as it makes the assumption that the character's environment contains enemies.

```
IF
    !Range(NearestEnemyOf(Myself),3)
    Range(NearestEnemyOf(Myself),8)
THEN
    RESPONSE #40
    EquipMostDamagingMelee()
    AttackReevalutate(NearestEnemyOf(Myself),60)
    RESPONSE #80
    EquipRanged()
    AttackReevalutate(NearestEnemyOf(Myself),30)
END
```

Fig. 1.3 An example rule from a warrior character in *Baldur's Gate* [11].

```
startup state Startup${
    trigger OnGoHandleMessage$(WE_ENTERED_WORLD){
        if (godb.IsEditMode()){
            SetState Finish$;
        }
        else{
            SetState Spawn$;
        }
    }
}

state Spawn${
    event OnEnterState${
        GoCloneReq cloneReq$ = MakeGoCloneReq(
          "gpg_gremal_caged" );
        cloneReq$.StartingPos = owner.Go.Placement.Position;
        cloneReq$.SetStartingOrient =
          owner.Go.Placement.Orientation;
        cloneReq$.SnapToTerrain = true;
        newGoid$ = GoDb.SCloneGo( cloneReq$ );
    }
    event OnGoHandleMessage$(eWorldEvent e$, WorldMessage msg$){
        ...
        Goid Master$;
        Master$ = msg$.GetSendFrom();
        if(master$.Go.Actor.GetSkillLevel("Combat Magic") > 0.01){
            Report.SScreen(master$.Go.Player.MachineId,
            Report.Translate(owner.go.getmessage("too_evil")));
        }
        else{
            ...
        }
    }
}

state Finish${
}
```

Fig. 1.4 An example of part of a state machine for a *Dungeon Siege* Gremel [12].

State Machines

State machines can be used to divide a NPC's reasoning process into a set of internal states and transitions. In the *Dungeon Siege* RPG, for example, each state contains a number of `event` constructs that cause actions to be taken based on the state of the game world. Triggers define when the NPC should transition to another internal state. An example of part of a state machine for a beast called a 'Gremel' [12] is shown in Fig. 1.4. As only characters that multiply would require a spawn state, this example shows how the states are character-dependent. In addition, the condition components of the rules within the states are again heavily domain-dependent – assuming for example that the environment contains characters that have a combat magic attribute.

Fuzzy Logic

Fuzzy logic provides a way to infer a conclusion based on facts that may be vague, ambiguous, inaccurate or incomplete [2]. *Close Combat 2* is an example of a game using fuzzy logic. Fuzzy logic uses fuzzy rules of the form `if <X is A> then <Y is B>`. X and Y are linguistic variables representing characteristics being measured – such as temperature, speed or height – while A and B represent fuzzy categories – such as hot, fast or tall. Fuzzy categories define decision thresholds within which certain courses of action may be pursued. Fuzzy logic can be applied to both rule-based approaches and state machines. While fuzzy logic allows characters to reason in environments where there is uncertainty, the ability of characters to adapt is still limited by the set of predefined fuzzy rules.

An extension of fuzzy logic is fuzzy state machines used in multiplayer simulation games such as *The Sims*. Fuzzy state machines combine state machine and fuzzy logic technologies to create agents that can identify and respond to states that approximately meet some predefined conditions [13]. For example, where simulation game NPCs controlled by state machines may consider balls as a target for kicking, NPCs controlled by fuzzy state machines may consider any object that, within some threshold, fits the description of 'being round' as a target for kicking. Characters with different personalities can be defined by building fuzzy state machines with different decision thresholds.

While fuzzy state machines have been used with success in existing simulation games, the need to define states and thresholds before the character is introduced to its environment limits the character to action within the predefined boundaries of states and decision thresholds. This technology thus becomes problematic in environments that can be modified in an open-ended manner.

In a departure from purely reflexive techniques, the support characters in some RPGs, such as *Blade Runner*, have simple goals. However these have also tended to be fairly narrow, supported by only a limited set of behaviours. Motivated reinforcement learning (MRL) offers an alternative to the design of fixed rule sets, states or goals in which a single agent model can be used to achieve multiple different characters, based on their experiences in their environment.

Flocking

Flocking [14] is a special example of rule-based reasoning used to control groups of characters such as crowds or animals. Flocking uses three rules governing the separation, alignment and cohesion of individuals in a flock, herd or other kind of group. Separation rules steer an individual to avoid others, alignment rules steer an individual towards the average heading of the flock and cohesion rules steer an individual towards the average position of the flock. Flocking algorithms have been used with great success to represent lifelike crowd and animal movement and have been incorporated in games such as *Half-Life* and *Unreal*. Using the basic flocking rules, flocks can adapt to changes in their environment by moving around, towards or away from objects. However, flocking does not allow character individuality or more complex adaptation.

1.3.2   Learning Agents

Learning agents are able to modify their internal structure in order to improve their performance with respect to some task [15]. In some games such as *Black and White*, NPCs can be trained to learn behaviours specified by their human master. The human provides the NPC with a reward such as food or patting to encourage desirable behaviour and punishment to discourage unwanted actions. While the behaviour of these characters may potentially evolve in any direction desired by the human, behaviour development relies on reward from human players, making it inappropriate for characters such as enemies or support characters. Learning algorithms used in games include decision trees, neural networks and reinforcement learning.

Decision Trees

Decision trees are hierarchical graphs learned from a training set of previously made decisions [16]. Internal nodes in the tree represent conditions about states of the environment, while leaf nodes represent actions. If all conditions on the path to a leaf node are fulfilled, the corresponding action can be taken. In *Black and White,* for example, creatures can learn decision trees about what food to eat based on how tasty the creature finds previously eaten food provided by a human player. While decision trees allow characters to learn, thus permitting more adaptable characters than reflexive approaches, they require a set of examples from which to learn. These examples must be provided by players. While this is appropriate for partner characters, it is generally inappropriate for enemies and support characters to have their behaviour determined only by players.

Neural Networks

Artificial neural networks comprise a network of computational neurons with interconnecting pathways [16]. Neural networks, like decision trees, learn from examples. Examples of correct actions in different situations are fed into the network to train a character. When a character encounters a similar situation it can make a decision about the correct action to take based on the data stored in the neural network. Neural networks are used by characters in games such as *Battlecruiser: 3000 AD*, but, in many cases, the neural network is frozen before the release of a game to prevent further learning during the game. Further learning from character actions can produce networks that adapt erratically or unpredictably to players' actions.

Reinforcement Learning

Researchers from *Microsoft* have shown that it is possible to use reinforcement learning (RL) [17] to allow NPCs to develop a single skill by applying it to fighting characters for the *Xbox* game, *Tao Feng* [18]. RL agents learn from trial-and-error and reward. After each interaction with its environment, a RL agent receives an input that contains some indication of the current state of the environment and the value of that state to the agent. This value is called a reward signal. The agent records the reward signal by updating a behavioural policy that represents information about the reward received in each state sensed so far. The agent then chooses an action that attempts to maximise the long-run sum of the values of the reward signal. In *Tao Feng*, while NPCs using RL can adapt their fighting techniques over time, it is not possible for them to identify new skills to learn about as they are limited by a pre-programmed reward for fighting. MRL offers an alternative approach for the design of learning characters that overcomes this limitation.

1.3.3   Evolutionary Agents

Evolutionary approaches such as genetic algorithms [19] simulate the process of biological evolution by implementing concepts such as natural selection, reproduction and mutation. Individuals in a population are defined in terms of a digital chromosome. When individuals reproduce, offspring are defined by a combination of their parent's chromosomes via processes of crossover and mutation. Offspring are then evaluated using a fitness function to determine which will remain in the population and which will be removed (die). Evolutionary algorithms are robust search methods that can optimise complex fitness functions. However, when genetic algorithms are used in NPCs, fitness functions must be predefined by game designers. As in RL, the fitness function limits the adaptability of a given population of individuals to the skills or tasks defined by the fitness function.

1.3.4   Smart Terrain

A key paradigm to arise from simulation games is the smart terrain concept developed by Will Wright for *The Sims* [11]. Smart terrain discards the character-oriented approach to reasoning using artificial intelligence and embeds the behaviours and possible actions associated with a virtual object within the object itself. For example, the file for the model of a television in *The Sims* might contain the instructions for watching it, turning it on and off, the conditions under which a 'Sim' might want to watch it and how a Sim should be animated while watching it. This approach allows new objects to be inserted into the game at any point, either as an expansion pack by game designers or using content creation tools by players. Achieving character adaptability using this approach, however, requires character behaviours to be explicitly programmed in each new object. This requires development effort from game designers and, while compelling for some gamers, is not interesting for others.

Expansion packs and content creation tools in general are approaches by which game designers have attempted to extend the lifetime of games by extending or allowing players to extend the original game through the addition of new content. Games in which open-ended modification of the game world is allowed while the game is in progress have the potential for a longer lifetime though the provision of more open-ended game play.

1.4 Summary

Multiuser games and open-ended virtual worlds are starting to be used for a broad range of activities, going beyond entertainment, which can be enhanced and supported by believable and adaptable NPCs. The in-world object modelling and programming capacity of virtual worlds such as *Second Life* provides a way for players to create and modify both the structure of virtual terrain, and the geometry, media content, and behaviour of world artefacts. This significantly changes players' expectations for believable NPCs and there is now a need for NPCs that can adapt to open-ended changes to their environment. In future the roles undertaken by NPCs in virtual worlds may also expand to encompass facilitators or arbitrators as well as traditional roles such as enemies and partners. This creates a need for new kinds of character control technology to enable NPCs to be capable of these more complex roles.

Current artificial intelligence approaches to developing the behaviour of NPCs include preprogrammed reflexive behaviours using techniques such as rules and state machines, and learned behaviours using techniques such as neural networks and reinforcement learning. The approaches have limitations in open-ended virtual worlds because they require specific knowledge embedded in the code about the state of the world and goals of the NPC. Using these techniques as a starting point, new learning approaches that include motivation as a trigger have the potential to create a new kind of NPC that is curious about the changes in the environment and is self-motivated to learn more about the changes.

This book introduces MRL as a new technique that transforms the design of NPCs by providing individual NPCs with a mechanism for open-ended, online adaptation of their own behaviour. The aim of this book is to provide game programmers with the knowledge required to develop adaptable, intelligent NPCs that can take on a life of their own in dynamic, multiuser virtual worlds. We begin in the next chapter by examining human motivation with a view to understanding how it can be embodied in artificial agents to achieve self-motivated, adaptive NPCs.

1.5 References

[1]   R. Bartle, Designing virtual worlds, New Riders, Indianapolis, 2004.

[2]   P. Baillie-de Byl, Programming believable characters for computer games, Charles River Media, Hingham, Massachusetts, 2004.

[3]   J. Laird and M. van Lent, Human-level AI's killer application: interactive computer games. AI Magazine, pp. 15–25, Summer 2001.

[4] D. Zeltzer, Autonomy, interaction and presence. Presence: Teleoperators and
     Virtual Environments 1(1):127–132, 1992.

[5] Linden, Second Life, www.secondlife.com (Accessed January, 2007).

[6] Active Worlds, www.activeworlds.com (Accessed January, 2007).

[7] There.com www.there.com (Accessed July, 2008).

[8] F. Rex, LambdaMOO: An introduction, http://www.lambdamoo.info (Accessed
     December, 2006).

[9] K. Merrick and M.L. Maher, Motivated reinforcement learning for adaptive
     characters in open-ended simulation games, ACM SIGCHI International
     Conference on Advances in Computer Entertainment Technology (ACE 2007),
     ACM, Salzburg, Austria, pp. 127–134, 2007.

[10] M.L. Maher and J.S. Gero, Agent models of 3D virtual worlds, ACADIA 2002:
     Thresholds, California State Polytechnic University, Pamona, pp. 127–138, 2002.

[11] S. Woodcock, Games making interesting use of artificial intelligence techniques.
     http://www.gameai.com/games.html (Accessed October, 2005).

[12] Siege University, 303 Skrit, http://garage.gaspowered.com (Accessed March,
     2006).

[13] D. Johnson and J. Wiles, Computer games with intelligence, The Tenth IEEE
     International Conference on Fuzzy Systems, pp. 1355–1358, 2001.

[14] C. Reynolds, Flocks, herds and schools: a distributed behavioural model.
     Computer Graphics 21(4):25–34, 1987.

[15] N.J. Nilsson, Introduction to machine learning,
     http://ai.stanford.edu/people/nilsson/mlbook.html (Accessed January, 2006), 1996.

[16] S.J. Russell and P. Norvig, Artificial intelligence: a modern approach, Prentice
     Hall, Englewood Cliffs, New Jersey, 1995.

[17] R.S. Sutton and A.G. Barto, Reinforcement learning: an introduction, The MIT
     Press Cambridge, Massachusetts, London, England, 2000.

[18] T. Graepel, R. Herbrich and J. Gold, Learning to fight, The International
     Conference on Computer Games: Artificial Intelligence, Design and Education,
     2004.

[19] D. Goldberg, Genetic algorithms, Addison-Wesley, Reading, Massachusetts,
     1989.

Chapter 2
Motivation in Natural and Artificial Agents

Motivation is "the reason one has for acting or behaving in a particular way". Motivation in humans has been studied from many different perspectives: biological, psychological, social, and so on. In contrast, motivation in artificial systems is a relatively new idea. In order to use motivation as a basis for designing adaptive characters that can evolve in complex, dynamic virtual environments, we consider models of motivation that are inspired by concepts from both natural systems and artificial intelligence. Specifically, theories from the psychological study of motivation are used as the basis for designing agents that can adapt by exhibiting problem-finding behaviour; that is, identifying new tasks on which to focus their attention. Computational models of motivation are combined with models of reinforcement learning [1] from the field of machine learning to develop agents that can adapt to new problems by learning.

As background and inspiration for motivated reinforcement learning models, this chapter reviews the theories of motivation proposed by psychologists as the cause of action in natural systems. Where they exist, the corresponding computational models of motivation for artificial agents are also reviewed with consideration given to how they might be applied to focus attention in non-player characters and reinforcement learning.

2.1 Defining Motivation

From a psychological perspective, motivation is defined as "the cause of action" in natural systems [2]. A natural system is one that has evolved in the natural environment and has not been artificially produced or changed by humans. Motivation in natural systems is thought to have three primary functions [3, 4]:

K.E. Merrick, M.L. Maher, *Motivated Reinforcement Learning*, DOI 10.1007/978-3-540-89187-1_2,
© Springer-Verlag Berlin Heidelberg 2009

- a directing function that focuses an individual's behaviour towards or away from specific goals;

- an activating function that energises action in pursuit of goals;

- an organising function that influences the combination of behavioural components into coherent, goal-oriented behavioural sequences.

Motivation theorists do not agree on a unified causal explanation of the behaviour of natural systems. Rather, causation has been attributed to such factors as the environment, physiology, the psyche or social forces, with many researchers tending to focus on one or the other of these views. Various attempts have been made to either classify [2, 3] or synthesise [5, 6] the large body of research related to psychological motivation. For example, Maslow's Hierarchy of Needs [6] was one of the first unified theories. Maslow [6] posited that human needs, and thus human motivations, occur in order from the most basic physiological and safety needs, through a series of love and esteem needs, to complex needs for self-actualisation. While the Hierarchy of Needs has strong intuitive appeal, experimental evidence has provided only mixed support for this theory.

Another approach is to classify rather than combine different psychological motivation theories. Geen et al. [3] categorise motivation theories as physiological, behavioural or social. Physiological theories emphasise the biological factors involved in the direction, intensity and persistence of behaviour. Behavioural theories are closely associated with processes such as learning, perception and cognitive organisation while social motivation is the study of interpersonal behaviour. Mook [2] takes the view that motivation theories are behaviourist, mediationist or biological. According to this categorisation, behaviourist motivation theories reject all explanations of action in terms of internal events such as thoughts and desires. Rather, they seek to explain action in terms of influences from the outside environment. The mediationist point of view can be divided into two classes. Psychodynamic views emphasise urges or impulses arising from within an individual. Cognitive views emphasise the thinking, judging, rational processes that in turn lead to action. Biological theories may cut across the boundaries of the previous two groups and can also be divided into two classes. Physiological theories describe how urges, environmental impacts or cognitions are translated into action by the physiological machinery of the body. Evolutionary theories describe causation in terms of a species' evolution of a repertoire of reflexes, instinctive action patterns and mechanisms of perceiving, leaning and thinking.

Computational models of motivation, perhaps as a result of the broad spectrum of psychological theories, have also tended to focus on individual aspects of motivation. Some computational models of motivation have been closely informed by psychological research, while others introduce new ideas specifically tailored to artificial systems. To classify motivation theories in a manner that is relevant for both natural and artificial systems, we consider four broad categories: biological, cognitive, social and combined motivation theories and models.

Motivation theorists agree about the existence of motivation processes that work within the biological system of a behaving organism. Biological motivations include physiological, safety or existence needs. In artificial systems, the biological organism is replaced with a hardware or software framework that supports reasoning. Computational models of motivation based on biological theories create artificial systems with some of the essential properties of life. Biological motivation theories for natural and artificial systems are discussed in Sect. 2.2.

Cognitive motivation, a second broad category, covers motivation theories of the mind that are abstracted from the biological system of the behaving organism. Cognitive motivation theories, discussed in Sect. 2.3, include the need for self-actualisation or relatedness and growth needs. This category is the focus of the artificial intelligence research community that seeks to achieve a scientific understanding of the mechanisms underlying thought and intelligent behaviour in order to embody them in machines. In artificial systems this embodiment is achieved through abstract computational structures such as states, goals, and actions that form the basis of cognitively inspired computational models of motivation.

The third category, social motivation theories, discussed in Sect. 2.4, covers theories of motivation concerned with what individuals do when they are in contact with one another. It includes love and esteem needs, social theories and evolutionary and cultural effect theories. Social motivation theories are recognised by both artificial life and artificial intelligence researchers, frequently informing the design of multiagent systems.

Combined motivation theories, discussed in Sect. 2.5, cover motivation theories that synthesise ideas from several of the previous categories. Combined motivation theories include Maslow's Hierarchy of Needs [6] and Alderfer's [5] Existence Relatedness Growth (ERG) theory. These theories attempt to represent an ideal for psychological theories, a unified theory of causality for natural systems. As our understanding of natural systems improves, new computational models are possible that capture increasingly more of the capabilities of natural systems. This permits the design of artificial systems that exhibit increasingly complex, realistic and believable behaviour for applications such as non-player characters in games.

2.2 Biological Theories of Motivation

Biological motivation theories explain motivation in terms of the processes that work at a biological level in natural systems. These theories often have a mechanistic quality in that they tend to explain behaviour in terms of energies and drives that push an organism towards certain behaviour. Existing artificial systems research has used computational models of biological motivation theories to create software agents and simulations of natural systems. These include simulation of animal behaviour and predator–prey simulations. Biological motivation theories are thus relevant to the design of non-player characters such as enemies – which have a predator–prey relationship with player characters – and support characters such as animal herds.

2.2.1   Drive Theory

The drive theory of motivation holds that homeostatic requirements drive an individual to restore some optimal biological condition when stimulus input is not congruous with that condition. For example, high body temperature might drive an individual to sweat in order to restore its optimal body temperature. Drive theory was developed in its most elaborate and systematic way by Hull as a central part of his theory of behaviour [7, 8]. Drive theory postulates that behaviour is a response both to a motivational factor called drive and to habits that are reinforced during an individual's lifetime. The more often a response is reinforced, the more habitual it becomes in a particular situation and the more likely it is to be repeated when the conditions are the same as those in which it was reinforced. When a response has become a habit through frequent reinforcement it comes to be performed more intensely under conditions of high drive. Drive theory models the relationship between habit, drive and a behavioural response as multiplicative:

Tendency for a behavioural response = Habit **x** *Drive*

The assumption that habit and drive strength multiply is based on the assumption that both are necessary for behaviour. If one is not present, that is, has zero strength, the resulting response potential will be zero.

Natural fluctuations in physiological variables such as body temperature or hormone levels drive the behaviour of natural systems in rhythmic biological cycles ranging from minutes to years. Cycles such as the sleep–wake cycle or hibernation are influenced by external variables such as temperature and light while other cycles such as mating behaviour or the menstrual cycle are controlled internally by hormones. The secretion of different hormones drives the emergence of different behaviours during different periods of each cycle.

Drive-based approaches have been studied in the artificial life community as an approach to building action selection architectures [9, 10, 11]. Action selection architectures for autonomous agents make decisions about what behaviours to execute in order to satisfy internal goals and guarantee an agent's continued functioning in a given environment. Motivations in action selection architectures are characterised by a set of controlled essential physiological variables, a set of drives to increase or decrease the level of the various controlled variables, a set of external incentive stimuli that can increase a motivation's intensity and a behavioural tendency of approach or avoidance towards these stimuli. A reward detector generates an error signal, the drive, when the value of a physiological variable departs from its set-point. This triggers the execution of preprogrammed inhibitory and excitatory behaviours to adjust the variable in the appropriate direction. Each motivation receiving an error signal from its reward detector receives an intensity or activation level proportional to the magnitude of the error.

Canamero [10] concludes that drive-based approaches to the design of action selection architectures can produce artificial agents fit to function in dynamic environments. These agents are characterised by the ability to make rapid choices that lead to both the satisfaction of long-term goals, as well as opportunistic behaviour to take advantage of immediate situations.

Many of the approaches to drive-based models by the artificial life community use physiological variables such as adrenaline, blood sugar and blood pressure that correspond directly to those found in natural systems. This allows artificial life researchers to simulate some of the essential properties of natural systems. However other approaches replace physiological variables with problem-specific motives to extend drive-based systems to other domains [12, 13, 14, 15]. Norman and Long [14] proposed a model for motivated goal creation that enables agents to create goals both reactively and proactively. In their model, the state of the environment and the agent are monitored by a set of motives. Motives are domain specific so, for a character taking the role of a warehouse manager for example, motives include satisfying orders in a timely manner, keeping the warehouse tidy and maintaining security. A change in state may trigger a response from the character agent if the strength of the motive exceeds a certain threshold. The strength of a motive is calculated from the state of the domain and the internal state of the agent. This mechanism ensures that the agent will only respond to and reason about changes if they are sufficiently important. A motivational response creates a goal to consider the primary reasons for the trigger of attention. If further activity is required a goal is created that will, if satisfied, cause the mitigation of the stimuli that triggered the motivation. This mitigation takes the form of planned actions in the agent's domain. Because these agents can predict their future beliefs they are able to create proactive goals.

Luck and d'Inverno [13] also proposed a system for motivated goal generation. Their system requires a goal-base populated with a set of possible goals. The motivation process returns a numeric value representing the motivational effect of satisfying a subset of goals from the goal-base. If there is a subset of goals in the goal-base that has a greater motivational effect than any other set of goals, then the current goals of the agent are updated to include the new goals. Current goals can be destroyed if the motivational effect of destroying them is greater than the effect of satisfying them.

Methods based on physiological or domain-specific variables represent two extremes for drive-based approaches to motivation in artificial systems. The former uses variables based directly on those found in nature for simulating biological systems. This approach appears promising for simulating adaptive non-player characters such as animals, birds or fish. The latter uses domain-specific motives to create goal oriented artificial systems, but, in fixing domain dependent motives, loses an essential characteristic of natural systems: their ability to adapt to new situations that were not predicted by the system designer.

2.2.2 Motivational State Theory

In recent years there has been a tendency by psychologists to drop the concept of drive, in particular because it is no longer believed that drives can be considered as unitary variables [16]. The notion of high or low hunger, for example, is a misnomer. Hunger is more accurately described in terms of a number of variables such as fat, protein and carbohydrates. One alternative to drive theory is the idea of a motivational state [16, 17]. An individual's motivational state can be represented by a point in a motivational space as shown in Fig. 2.1. The axes of the space are important motivational stimuli such as fat or protein levels or the strength of some external stimulus. The major difference between the state-space approach to motivation and the drive concept is that the state-space approach makes no assumption that different motivational factors are multiplicative or about the relationship between motivation and behaviour.

Motivational state theory can be thought of as a generalisation of drive theory that extends one-dimensional drives to multidimensional motivational states. While existing artificial systems research has used the simpler drive-based model as a starting point, motivational state theory also has the potential for development as a computational model of motivation. Because this approach allows for more accurate representation of motivational state in terms of multiple variables, it has the potential to offer greater power of expression for the design of artificial systems than using a drive-based approach. For example, rather than expressing an individual's energy level as a single

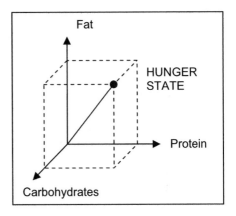

Fig. 2.1 Motivational state theory describes hunger more accurately than drive theory by using multiple motivational variables [17].

variable, energy may be expressed in terms of various different variables that connect the individual to its environment. These may include exposure to the sun, water sources, and food sources.

2.2.3 Arousal

In both drive and motivational state theories, a total absence of homeostatic drives such as hunger or thirst should produce an individual that does, and seeks to do, nothing. However, studies of sensory deprivation and isolation in the early 1950s showed that low levels of stimulation, which should produce little drive and hence be attractive according to drive theory, are in fact unattractive and produce a tendency to seek out stimulus complexity. Arousal theory offers an alternative to drive theory's explanation of the intensive aspects of behaviour by stating that individuals seek from their environment, not a universally minimal amount of stimulation, but rather a moderate or optimal level of stimulation so there is an inverted U-shaped relationship between the intensity of a stimulus and its pleasantness [18]. Berlyne [19, 20] further decomposed this relationship into the joint action of positive and negative reward to a stimulus as shown in Fig. 2.2.

One model for the conditions that produce arousal assumes that arousal is a response to a change in the level of stimulation to which an individual is exposed between an existing condition of stimulation and a new and different condition [3]. Implicit in the idea of an existing state is the assumption that individuals tend to establish a baseline level of stimulation through constant adjustments and adaptations to their environment. Over time a loss of sensitivity accrues with prolonged exposure to a particular stimulus. This process is called habituation.

As with motivational state theory, arousal theory has been largely ignored with respect to the development of biologically inspired computational models of motivation. Unlike drive theory, that pushes individuals to reduce drives and maintain internal stability, arousal theory pushes individuals to maintain a level of internal stimulation. In artificial systems, the use of such an approach has the potential to permit systems with different personality characteristics and behavioural responses to drive-based approaches.

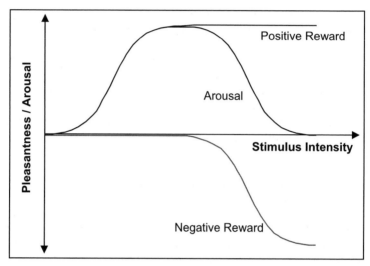

Fig. 2.2 Arousal results from the joint action of positive and negative reward for a stimulus [20, 21].

The decomposition of arousal into positive and negative reward has proved highly flexible and has had great appeal for cognitive theories of motivation in both natural and artificial system theory. Berlyne [21] used this model to extend arousal theory to the cognitive concepts of curiosity and exploratory behaviour and similar relationships apply to other cognitively based psychological theories such as achievement and intrinsic motivation discussed in Sect. 2.3. The development of computational models of interest, curiosity and creativity in artificial systems has also been informed by Berlyne's model of curiosity. Likewise, the role of habituation in establishing a baseline level of stimulation has also influenced the development of computational models of novelty [22].

Easterbrook [23] proposed that arousal also has the effect of restricting the focus of attention by reducing the range of cues that are utilised in performance. In ordinary functioning, individuals do not respond equally to all the stimuli that impinge upon them. Instead, they attend to some stimuli more than others. Sperber and Wilson [24] write that the stimuli to which an agent attends are the ones an individual considers to be relevant. Because of the difficulties of developing artificial systems for complex environments, theories of attention focus have been a key research direction for artificial systems. Attention focus describes the process by which an artificial agent limits the information about which it must reason by selecting important aspects of its current experience and memory to which it need attend [25]. In complex environments, a sensed state may contain large amounts of information, not all of which is relevant to the tasks that an agent is performing. In addition to large sensed states, if an environment is dynamic, data stored in the agent's memory may become obsolete over time. Thus, focus of attention is an important consideration for designing agent reasoning processes that are scalable in complex, dynamic environments.

Fonar and Maes [25] describe the different types of attention focus that might be required by artificial agents in terms of perceptual and cognitive selectivity. The process of limiting the sensations attended to at a given time is called perceptual selectivity. The process of limiting the internal structures that are considered when acting and learning is called cognitive selectivity. Perceptual and cognitive selectivity may be either domain-dependent or domain-independent. Domain-independent methods represent general heuristics for focus of attention that can be employed in any environment. Conversely, domain-dependent heuristics are specific to the current environment of the agent.

Attention focus methods may also be either goal-driven or world-driven. World-driven attention focus determines which sensory or memory bits are 'generally' ignored. Goal-driven attention focus determines which sensory or memory bits are ignored only some of the time when a particular task is being performed. Finally, attention focus may be either spatial or temporal. Spatial selectivity limits the focus of attention in the world state dimension by ignoring certain sensations in the current sensed state. In contrast, temporal selectivity limits the focus of attention by restricting the time period over which an agent attends to stored data.

Theories of attention focus have been implemented in various artificial systems, including reinforcement learning (RL) systems, in a number of different ways. In RL for example, techniques such as function approximation using decision trees achieve cognitive selectivity by representing policies using only the most discriminating features of the sensed state. The models in this book, in contrast, are concerned with achieving a form of adaptive perceptual selectivity by using motivation to focus attention on different subsets of the state and action space at different times.

2.3 Cognitive Theories of Motivation

The view of hunger and thirst as homeostatic drives or the notion optimal arousal theory imply that eating, drinking or exploration are initiated as a result of monitored changes in physiological state. However, in addition to occurring in response to physiological changes, behaviours such as feeding and drinking often occur in anticipation of such changes [16]. In recognition of this, cognitive motivation theories focus on questions such as what determines the consequences of behaviour, how consequences influence behaviour and to what extent individuals account for the probable consequences of future behaviour in terms of the costs and benefits of different courses of actions. Cognitive theories of motivation offer a starting point from which computational models of motivation based on abstract machine learning and artificial intelligence concepts such as goals, plans and policies can be developed.

2.3.1 Curiosity

Berlyne [20] extended arousal theory to the cognitive concepts of curiosity and exploratory behaviour by suggesting that such behaviours may have two types, diversive and specific exploration, both motivated by a need to bring stimulation nearer to some optimal level. Diversive exploration is a reaction to under-stimulation and boredom. An individual becomes habituated to its surroundings, experiences boredom and is uncomfortable. To bring the arousal level nearer to the optimum, the individual seeks out new stimuli to replace the habituated ones. Specific exploration occurs in an over-stimulated individual to lower arousal by seeking out familiar or simple stimulation. When over-stimulation occurs, an individual can select certain stimuli for attention and ignore the remainder, thus achieving a stimulation level that is optimal for pleasure and performance. Habituation and recovery influence the formation of behavioural cycles at the cognitive level. As behavioural responses habituate, an individual is motivated to seek a more optimal level of stimulation. This change in behaviour allows the original behaviour to recover to the extent that it may become optimally stimulating again at some future time, resulting in behavioural cycles. Psychological models of habituation and curiosity have, to different degrees, informed the development of a number of models of novelty and interest.

Marsland et al. [22] used Stanley's model of habituation [26] to implement a real-time novelty detector for mobile robots. Like the Kohonen Novelty Filter [27], a real-time novelty detector uses a Self-Organising Map (SOM) as the basis for the detection of novelty. Habituation and recovery extends a novelty filter with the ability to forget. This allows a more realistic approach to stimuli that occur only infrequently. Using a real-time novelty detector, such stimuli are always considered novel rather than learned over time.

Saunders and Gero [28, 29] drew on the work of Berlyne [20] and Marsland et al. [22] to develop computational models of curiosity and interest based on novelty. They used a real-time novelty detector to implement novelty. However, they state that novelty is not the only determinant of interest. Rather, interest in a situation is also related to how well an agent can learn the information gained from novel experiences. Consequently, the most interesting experiences are often those that are 'similar-yet-different' to previously encountered experiences. Saunders and Gero [28] model interest using sigmoid functions to represent positive reward for the discovery of novel stimuli and negative reward for the discovery of highly novel stimuli. The resulting computational models of novelty and interest are used in a range of applications including curious agents. Curious social force agents extend the social force model [30] with a fifth force, a desire to move towards potentially interesting physical locations. Curious social force agents can exhibit complex behaviour that changes over time with exposure to new experiences. Saunders and Gero [31] also used a combination of neural networks to represent novelty with RL to create curious design agents.

In different approaches, Schmidhuber also defined a number of computational models of interest for use in RL systems. One such model [32] uses the predictability of a learned world model to represent curiosity and boredom as reinforcement and pain units. Predictability is measured as the result of classifying sequential observations using a self-supervised neural network. The resulting Curious Neural Controller works in conjunction with RL and is designed to reward situations where the model network's prediction performance is not optimal, in order to encourage an agent to revisit those situations and improve its network model. As in Berlyne's [21] theory, maximum motivational reward is generated for moderate levels of predictability to represent curiosity about situations in which an 'ideal mismatch' occurs between what is expected and what is observed. This reward process is designed to represent the theory that a system cannot learn something that it does not already almost know.

Various other computational models of interest also exist that depart further from psychological models of curiosity. For example, Lenat's AM [33] included forty-three heuristics designed to assess what is interesting. Schmidhuber [34] also created a curious, creative explorer with two co-evolving brains as a model of interest. Oudyer and Kaplan [35, 36] developed Intelligent Adaptive Curiosity (IAC) as a motivation systems for robots that encourages attention focus on situations that maximise learning progress. They model IAC as a drive towards the maintenance of an abstract dynamic cognitive variable, the learning progress, which must be kept maximal. They refer to it as a cognitive model of curiosity as it pushes a robotic agent towards an abstract representation of situations in which it can learn. This model, and an earlier model on which it is based [37], is used in conjunction with a simple one-step, reward-based prediction learning algorithm similar to RL.

The proliferation of computational models of curiosity in artificial intelligence literature is possibly a result of the goals of many other types of artificial systems. Machine learning and planning systems, for example, aim to solve problems by various means. The association between curiosity and the exploratory behaviour required for successful problem solving makes computational models of curiosity – and the associated concepts of interest and novelty – a natural starting point. As such, the work of Saunders and Gero [31] and Kaplan and Oudeyer [35, 36, 37] provides inspiration for the models in this book. These models are discussed further in Chap. 3.

2.3.2   Operant Theory

Tolman [38] recognised that individuals are not only driven by deprivations and needs but may be guided to important goals by perceptions and cognitions. When an individual does something that is rewarded, it is not influenced by any real or imagined loss of drive but by the idea of being rewarded. A voluntary response emitted by an individual in order to achieve some reward is called an operant. Skinner's law of conditioning for operants [39] states that if the occurrence of an operant is followed by the presentation of a reward, the strength of the operant will be increased. The converse law, the law of extinction, states that if the occurrence of an operant already strengthened through conditioning is not followed by a reward, the strength is decreased. A reward is not assigned any specific properties other than that it follows an operant. For example, it may be a pleasant, internal feeling of satisfaction, the receipt of money from an external source, an unpleasant, internal feeling of boredom or an electric shock from an external source. Figure 2.3 shows how successful acquisition of reward triggers the formation of mental associations between acts and the rewards that follow them. This association in turn generates an expectancy that if the act is repeated it will be rewarded again. When a reward is no longer forthcoming an individual will still try to achieve it for some time until it learns that it cannot. Extinction of response follows soon after.

In artificial systems, operant theory is modelled by the RL paradigm [1]. The mental association between acts and the rewards that follow them is represented using structures such as a learned table, neural network or decision tree. As with natural systems, RL systems can display both reinforcement and extinction of a behavioural response. The RL framework [1] also presents an abstract notion of reward, suitable to represent both internal and external feedback following an operant. In practice, however, reward signals used in

RL have characteristically defined specific tasks chosen by system designers, external to the learning agent. As with the drive-based models of motivation that assume domain-dependent drives, the assumption that reinforcement signals define specific tasks again loses the key property of natural systems, that they are able to adapt to unpredictable situations. In addition, it requires that a reward signal be hand-crafted for each agent.

In large scale, multiuser virtual worlds, there may be hundreds of characters. Designing a reward signal for each character is time consuming, and limits the adaptability of characters. The models presented in this book return to the original psychological theory that the reward may itself be defined by a psychological model of motivation. This aim of this approach is to recapture the fundamental adaptability achieved by natural systems, and permit the design of a single agent model for multiple characters that may then evolve different behaviours based on their experiences in their environment. The computational theory underlying existing approaches to RL is discussed in detail in Chap. 3.

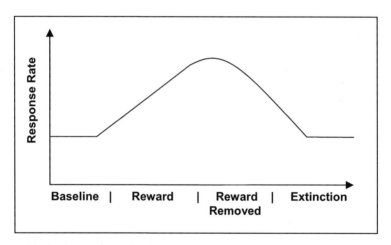

Fig. 2.3 Operant theory describes the relationship between reward and behaviour.

2.3.3 Incentive

In psychological theory, the expectancy of being rewarded after some responses forms the basis of incentive. The expectancy–value theory of incentive defines incentive in terms of expectancy and value of reward:

Incentive for a behavioural response =
Expectancy of reward x *Value of reward*

Mook [2] extends the notion of expectancy in his description of decision theory. The fundamental axiom of decision theory is the principle of maximisation. An individual performs the action, the imagined or expected outcome of which has the highest utility or operant strength. The term utility is borrowed from economics and is a neutral means of describing the strength of an operant. The expected utility of a behavioural response is defined in terms of its probable outcomes and their rewards:

$$Expected\ Utility = \sum_{Outcomes} (Expectancy\ of\ reward \times Value\ of\ reward)$$

The principle of maximisation states that an individual will choose the behavioural response that maximises expected utility. This is the underlying principle for action selection in artificial RL agents. However, where RL agents initially use task-oriented reward to assign utility, incentive theory looks to more generic approaches. Two different approaches are to define utility in terms of an individual's tendency to either approach success or avoid failure. These tendencies form the basis of the theory of achievement motivation.

2.3.4   Achievement Motivation

The dominant approach to achievement oriented motivation was formulated by Atkinson et al. [40, 41]. This theory, like the expectancy–value theory, is based on the expectancy of attaining a goal, the perceived value of the goal theorem and a third, relatively stable variable, the level of motivation. Motivation level multiplies with expectancy and value:

$$Incentive\ for\ a\ behavioural\ response =$$
$$Expectancy\ of\ reward \times Value\ of\ reward \times Motivation$$

The value of reward is defined in terms of either a tendency to approach success or a tendency to avoid failure. If an individual is motivated by a tendency to approach success, they will evaluate the potential reward of a situation in terms of their probability of success as follows:

$$Value\ of\ reward = 1 - Expectancy\ of\ reward$$

This means that success on a difficult task is more valuable than success on a simple one. Individuals motivated to achieve success tend to select tasks of moderate difficulty. The effect of the motivation variable on the incentive for a behavioural response in an individual motivated to achieve success is to make their tendency to select tasks of moderate difficulty more pronounced as shown in Fig. 2.4.

In addition to motivation levels, Raynor [42] proposed that future orientation can also have the effect of emphasising certain behavioural tendencies in individuals motivated to approach success. The principle of future orientation is that when an individual is highly motivated to achieve, performance will depend in part on the perceived long-term instrumentality of the immediate goal to success on later tasks. The effect of future orientation on the tendency to approach success may be conceptualised as additive across successive tasks in a chain. The greater the number of steps that must be completed before final realisation of the long-range goal, the greater the tendency to work at achieving any given one:

$$\textit{Incentive for a behavioural response} =$$
$$\sum_{\textit{Tasks}} \textit{Expectancy of reward} \times \textit{Value of reward} \times \textit{Motivation}$$

Some individuals, rather than being motivated to approach success, are motivated simply to avoid failure. If an individual is motivated by a tendency to avoid failure they will evaluate the potential reward of a situation as follows:

$$\textit{Value of reward} = - \textit{Expectancy of reward}$$

Thus, the higher the probability of achieving a task, the greater the negative incentive associated with failure at that task. Individuals motivated to avoid failure tend to choose either easy tasks at which they are likely to succeed or difficult tasks for which there is a clear reason for failure. The value of the motivation variable again makes this tendency more or less pronounced as shown in Fig. 2.4.

Motivation to succeed and motivation to avoid failure are two general approaches to utility in incentive theory and thus to reward in operant theory. As such, they suggest possible bases for computational models of motivation in RL systems. Such models would first define a computational model of task difficulty to which a computational model of achievement motivation could be applied.

2.3.5   Attribution Theory

While expectancies and values together determine an individual's orientation toward future behaviour, theories such as the expectancy–value theory of incentive do not explain how expectancies and values are formed. Rather an

Fig. 2.4 Incentive for behavioural
response in individuals with
differing motivational strength to
approach success or avoid
failure.

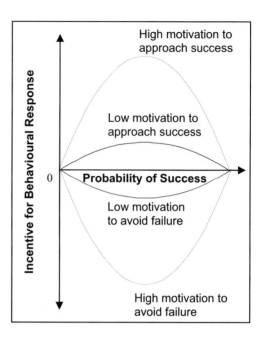

individual's cognitive representation of the environment and their role in it is
simply assumed to exist. Attribution theory seeks to provide this explanation.
A causal attribution is an inference about why some event has taken place. An
attribution may be about one's own behaviour or about another's behaviour.

Heider [43] introduced the idea that people follow specifiable rules in
interpreting the causes of behaviour. Attribution theory attempts to specify the
processes that are involved when an individual develops an explanation for the
behaviour of others or of themselves. Heider [43] used attribution theory to
develop his Naïve Analysis of Action theory that describes the cause of
behaviour in terms of the average person's commonsense analysis of
behaviour. Central to the Naïve Analysis of Action theory, shown
diagrammatically in Fig. 2.5, is the idea that both naïve perceivers and
professional psychologists share the belief that there are two classes of causes:
personal forces and environmental forces. Each of these forces is further
divided into two categories: 'ability' and 'trying', 'task difficulty' and 'luck',
respectively. The relationship between ability and task difficulty is defined to
be additive. That is, environmental forces could oppose or support the personal
force and thus increase or reduce its effectiveness. Furthermore, the personal
force trying is made up of two components: intention and exertion. Successful
action depends on the presence of both.

The division between personal and environmental forces provides
additional insight into the different types of computational models of
motivation that might exist. Existing computational models of novelty and

interest have tended to be extrospective, that is, they generate motivation values based on environmental forces such as stimuli from an agent's environment. The ability to introspect would allow agents to consider personal forces such as 'ability' and 'trying' when reasoning about how to act.

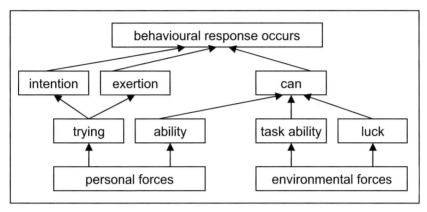

Fig. 2.5 The Naïve Analysis of Action Theory [43] divides motivational forces into two classes: personal forces and environmental forces.

2.3.6 Intrinsic Motivation

Attribution theory can produce an explanation for some behaviours in terms of personal forces such as physiological drives "because they are hungry" and environmental forces such as rewards "to earn money". However there are other behaviours that are inexplicable to the average observer. For example, some people make a pastime of skydiving "for fun" or climb mountains "because they are there". These behaviours involve exploration, seeking novelty, curiosity or meeting a challenge. The psychological terms for motivation inspiring such behaviour are intrinsic motivation, competence motivation and effectance motivation.

White [44] first argued for the existence of what he called effectance motivation or competence motivation. He proposed that individuals are motivated to engage in behaviours that can satisfy the desire to feel self-determining and competent. Effectance motivation is the desire to deal effectively with one's environment. It corresponds to the cognitive need to know, understand and explore in Maslow's needs hierarchy [6]. Like Maslow, White believes that effectance motivation is always present but is only manifested when other more basic needs are satisfied. Specifically, behaviours such as exploratory play, curiosity and stimulation seeking would be expected to appear only when an individual is otherwise homeostatically balanced. White [44] also proposed that effectance motivation is undifferentiated, meaning that the satisfaction of the effectance motive is not tied specifically to any given behaviour. Rather any behaviour that allows an individual to deal effectively with its surroundings can satisfy the motive.

Deci and Ryan [45] also proposed that intrinsic motivation be defined in terms of an individual's needs for competence and self-determination. They went further to define the types of behaviours that will permit an individual to gain a sense of competence and self-determination. They proposed that individuals are involved in an ongoing, cyclical process of seeking out or creating optimally challenging situations and then attempting to conquer those challenges. A feeling of competence emerges from situations in which an individual is optimally challenged. Optimally challenging situations are based on an individual's unique complement of skills. The situations that are most intrinsically motivating are those that contain information relevant to structures already stored and mastered but that are discrepant enough to call forth adaptive modifications. Overly familiar or excessively repetitive tasks and tasks that greatly exceed existing capacities will trigger boredom and distress respectively [46]. In other words, individuals will orient themselves towards an activity in some domain of behaviour where they are required to learn or stretch their abilities by a small amount, that is, tasks that are neither too difficult nor too easy.

In contrast to the psychological definition of intrinsic motivation by White [44] or Deci and Ryan [45], most of the computational models that refer to intrinsic motivation use the term to differentiate between task-oriented motivation provided by the system designer and experience-based motivation computed internally by an artificial agent. One such example is intrinsically motivated RL designed by Singh et al. [47] to produce agents that are able to develop a broad range of competencies in a wider range of domains. In this model, agents are programmed to identify changes in light and sound intensity as salient (interesting) events. Each first encounter with a salient event initiates learning a set of actions, or an option and an option-model [48], that when executed cause that event to occur. An intrinsic reward is generated each time the event is encountered that is proportional to the error in the prediction of the event according to the learned option-model for that event. When the agent encounters an unpredicted, salient event a few times, its updated action-value function drives it to repeatedly attempt to achieve that event. As the agent acts in the world, all the options and their models initiated so far are simultaneously updated using intra-option learning algorithms. Initially only the primitive actions in the environment are available to the agent. Over time, the agent identifies and learns skills represented by options and option models comprised of the primitive actions. These then become available to the agent as action choices. As the agent tries to achieve salient events, learning improves both in its policy for doing so and its option-model that predicts the event. As the option policy and option model improve, the intrinsic reward diminishes and the agent becomes bored with the associated event and seeks to achieve other salient events.

While the intrinsically motivated RL model of Singh et al. [47] contributes to models for multitask learning in RL settings, it does not provide a domain-independent model for autonomously defining motivation. In contrast, the psychological theory for intrinsic motivation offers a concise, domain and task independent theory on which a computational model of motivation could be based. Such a model would again use a computational model of task difficulty as a basis to which a computational model of optimal challenges could then be applied. We reserve the term 'intrinsic motivation' to refer to models based on psychological theories of motivation and refer to the Singh et al. [47] model of motivation with respect to reinforcement learning as 'motivated' RL.

2.4 Social Theories of Motivation

Social motivation theories are concerned with what individuals do when they are in contact with one another. Social theories of motivation cross the boundaries of biological and cognitive theories. Theories such as conformity and cultural effect, for example, describe cognitive phenomena, while the theory of evolution can be thought of as a biological social theory. Social motivation theories describe individuals in situations ranging from small groups to larger societies, cultures and evolutionary systems. These theories offer an important starting point for the design of computational models of motivation for multiagent systems.

2.4.1   Conformity

The term conformity refers to behaviour that an individual engages in because of a real or imagined group pressure. It must be different from what the individual might have done were the pressure not exerted. Research has shown that conformity pressures can be powerful and effective motivators in both small and large groups. One aspect of conformity lies in the role of social motivation in creative processes. Csikszentmihalyi's [49] theory of the triangular relationship between the creative person, the field and the domain says that the field plays some necessary and positive roles in the life of a highly creative person. In this context, the field comprises the individuals that are knowledgeable about the domain. In the early development of the creative person, the field introduces knowledge associated with the domain to a potentially creative person, trains the person in the skills relevant to the domain, and motivates the person by revealing the significance of the domain.

Later, the field provides the constructive criticism necessary for self-improvement and an audience for the person's creative contributions. Finally, it is the field that actually creates the reputation of the creative person and thereby brings that person to the attention of the general public.

Just as biological cycles emerge as a result of drives and more abstract behavioural cycles emerge as a result of habituation, social cycles can emerge as a result of the interaction between the individual and the group. Habituation and recovery can occur at a social as well as an individual level, influencing the focus of attention of large groups. Fashion cycles are one example of such cyclic behaviour at a social level.

Saunders and Gero [50] produced a computational model of creativity that captures social aspects of the search for novelty. In their model, agents can communicate particularly interesting artwork to others, as well as reward other agents for finding interesting artwork. They show that both an individual's need for novelty and the collective experience of a group of agents are responsible for creating a consensus as to what is creative.

2.4.2   *Cultural Effect*

The theory of cultural effect extends social motivation beyond groups to the wider social settings of a culture. Mook [2] holds that culture affects action in two ways. First, he writes that it determines what skills, thoughts and schemata are cognitively available to an individual in a particular situation. For example an individual from western society lost in a forest may not have the notion of eating ants as a means of satiating hunger. Secondly, Mook [2] notes that cultural values affect what selections an individual will make from those that are cognitively available. For example suppose someone informed the lost individual that ants are a good source of protein. The individual might still balk at eating them based on their cultural perception of ants as dirty or ugly.

2.4.3   *Evolution*

Charles Darwin's theory of evolution [51] contributes a different view of motivation. His idea was that animals have the structural and behavioural characteristics required to survive and to breed within their habitats. His theory has three key components. First, animals vary from one another within a species. Secondly, animals pass on their characteristics to their offspring. Thirdly, variation within a species means that some members of the species are better adapted than others to the ecology in which they live. Those better adapted are more likely to have offspring and pass on their structural and behavioural characteristics. Those that are poorly adapted will have fewer offspring so their characteristics will diminish over successive generations. Thus the cause of an individual's behaviour can be thought of as influenced by generations of the individual's ancestors and by the selection pressure by the environment in which the species lives.

In artificial systems, evolution is modelled by the large body of research concerned with genetic algorithms. Genetic algorithms are characterised by a society of individuals with computational models of chromosomes that can combine and mutate. A fitness function defines which individuals proceed to the next time step and pass on their structural or behavioural characteristics. Gusarev et al. [52] experimented with a population of motivated agents capable of reproducing. Their simulation consisted of a population of agents with two basic needs, the need for energy and the need to reproduce. The population evolves in an environment where patches of food grow. Agents can move, eat grass and mate with each other. Mating results in a new agent that inherits the characteristics of its parents according to some simple genetic rules. Their simulation demonstrated that simple hierarchical control systems in which simple reflexes are controlled by motivations, can emerge from evolutionary processes. They showed that this hierarchical system is more effective compared to behavioural control governed by means of simple reflexes only.

Evolutionary theories represent an important component of motivation models for artificial systems such as RL agents designed to function in dangerous environments. They allow adaptation to occur over generations of individuals so that the failure or destruction of a single individual can be tolerated and even used as a trigger for learning within the society as a whole.

2.5 Combined Motivation Theories

A small number of psychological motivation theories attempt to synthesise biological, cognitive and social motivation theories. These include Maslow's Hierarchy of Needs [6], ERG theory [5] and the steady state model [53]. While combined models of motivation for artificial systems are yet to become a research focus, they represent a goal towards which such models can aspire: comprehensive algorithms that describe the causes of action at the hardware, abstract reasoning and multiagent levels.

2.5.1 Maslow's Hierarchy of Needs

Maslow [6] attempted to unify the large body of research related to human motivation by defining a hierarchy of human needs as shown in Fig. 2.6. He posited that the most basic human needs are physiological needs such as hunger and thirst. Freedom from danger is the next need to emerge. When both physiological and safety needs are gratified, the needs arise to love and to be loved and thus to belong. If needs for love and friendship are met the need for the esteem of others emerges. When all the lower deficiency needs are met, higher level growth needs become a concern. The first of these is the cognitive need to know, understand and explore. When this is met the aesthetic need arises for symmetry, order and beauty. Finally, an individual will seek self-actualisation, the need to find self-fulfilment, and self-transcendence, the need to connect to something beyond the ego or to help others find self-fulfilment. Maslow's hierarchy of needs has parallels in Brooke's subsumption architecture [54] in which simple behaviours are subsumed by more complex ones. As such, a layered motivational hierarchy has the potential to provide a means of triggering subsumption within a behavioural hierarchy.

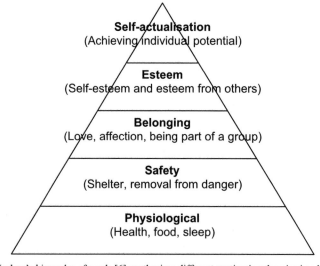

Fig. 2.6 Maslow's hierarchy of needs [6] synthesises different motivation theories in a hierarchy.

2.5.2 Existence Relatedness Growth Theory

While Maslow's Hierarchy of Needs [6] has strong intuitive appeal, especially in managerial settings, experimental evidence has provided only mixed support for his theory [2]. Several studies support the existence of two basic categories for deficiency needs and growth needs. However the existence of a strict ordering of needs is not well supported. In response to this lack of evidence, Alderfer [5] proposed a conceptually simpler framework know as Existence Relatedness Growth (ERG) theory, shown in Fig. 2.7. ERG theory proposes only three basic needs: existence, relatedness and growth. Existence needs correspond closely to Maslow's physiological and safety needs. Relatedness needs correspond to love needs. Growth needs correspond to Maslow's esteem and growth needs. Unlike Maslow, however, Alderfer [5] asserts that multiple needs may operate simultaneously and that there is no specific order in which needs are activated. Alderfer offers an alternative means of inspiration for the combination of different types of motivation in artificial systems.

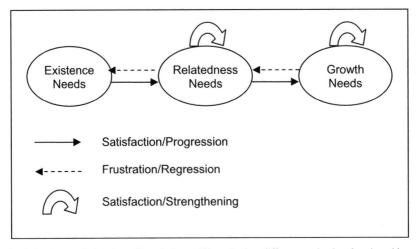

Fig. 2.7 Existence Relatedness Growth theory [5] synthesises different motivation theories without ordering.

2.6 Summary

Theories of motivation developed for natural systems describe the cause of action and attention focus in terms of biological, cognitive and social forces. These theories provide inspiration for the development of different types of artificial systems that display adaptive attention focus. These, in turn, are useful for different types of non-player characters. Biological motivation theories, for example, are relevant to the design of non-player characters such as enemies – which have a predator–prey relationship with player characters – and support characters such as animal herds.

Alternatively, cognitive theories of motivation move beyond the biological organism to abstract theories of the mind. Cognitive theories of motivation offer a starting point from which computational models of motivation based on abstract machine learning and artificial intelligence concepts such as goals, plans and policies can be developed. These are relevant to the design of humanoid characters capable of advanced planning or learning.

Other types of artificial systems, such as multiagent systems, are informed by social motivation theories that describe what individuals do when they are in contact with one another. Social motivation theories can thus inform the way that non-player characters should interact with each other and with player characters.

Finally, combined motivation theories take a unified approach to motivation and can be thought of as a long-term goal towards which computational models of motivation can aspire: comprehensive algorithms that describe the causes of action at the simulated biological, abstract reasoning and multiagent levels.

The models in this book are concerned specifically with the development of computational models of motivation to trigger adaptive, multitask learning in non-player characters. Cognitive motivation theories are identified as a starting point for such models, because these theories describe the abstract reasoning level relevant to the notion of a task and learning. The next chapter introduces the fundamentals of reinforcement learning, and studies the progression from reinforcement learning to motivated reinforcement learning.

2.7 References

[1] R.S. Sutton and A.G. Barto, Reinforcement learning: an introduction, The MIT Press Cambridge, Massachusetts, London, England, 2000.

[2] D.G. Mook, Motivation: the organization of action, W. W. Norton and Company, New York, 1987.

[3] R.G. Geen, W.W. Beatty and R.M. Arkin, Human motivation: physiological, behavioral and social approaches, Allyn and Bacon, Massachusetts, 1984.

[4] E.R. Kandel, J.H. Schwarz and T.M. Jessell, Essentials of neural science and behaviour, Appleton and Lang, Norwalk, 1995.

[5] C. Alderfer, Existence, relatedness and growth, Free Press, New York, 1972.

[6] A. Maslow, Motivation and personality, Harper, New York, 1954.

[7] C.L. Hull, Principles of behavior, Appleton-Century-Crofts, New York, 1943.

[8] C.L. Hull, A behavior system: an introduction to behavior theory concerning the individual organism, Yale University Press, New Haven, 1952.

[9]   O. Avila-Garcia and L. Canamero, Comparison of behaviour selection architectures using viability indicators, The EPSRC/BBSRC International Workshop on Biologically Inspired Robotics: The Legacy of W. Grey Walter, HP Labs, Bristol, UK, pp. 8–93, 2002.

[10] L. Canamero, Modelling motivations and emotions as a basis for intelligent behaviour. In: W.L. Johnson (Eds.), The First International Symposium on Autonomous Agents, ACM Press, New York, NY, pp. 148–155, 1997.

[11] C. Gershenson, Artificial Societies of Intelligent Agents, Engineering, Fundacion Arturo Rosenblueth, Mexico, 2001.

[12] R. Aylett, A. Coddington and G. Petley, Agent-based continuous planning, The 19th Workshop of the UK Planning and Scheduling Special Interest Group (PLANSIG 2000), 2000.

[13] M. Luck and M. d'Inverno, Motivated behaviour for goal adoption. In: C. Zhang and D. Lukose (Eds.), Multi-Agent Systems: Theories, Languages and Applications, Proceedings of the Fourth Australian Workshop on Distributed Artificial Intelligence, Springer-Verlag, pp. 58–73, 1998.

[14] T.J. Norman and D. Long, Goal creation in motivated agents, Intelligent agents: theories, architectures and languages, Springer-Verlag, pp. 277–290, 1995.

[15] M. Schmill and P. Cohen, A motivational system that drives the development of activity, AAMAS, ACM, Bologna, Italy, pp. 358–359, 2002.

[16] D. McFarland, Animal behaviour, Longman, England, 1995.

[17] D. Bindra, A unified account of classical conditioning and operant training. In: A. Black and W. Prokasy (Eds.), Classical conditioning – current theory and research, Appleton-Century-Crofts, New York, USA, pp. 453–481, 1974.

[18] W. Wundt, Principles of physiological psychology, Macmillan, New York, 1910.

[19] D.E. Berlyne, Novelty, complexity and hedonic value. Perception and Psychophysics 8:279–286, 1970.

[20] D.E. Berlyne, Aesthetics and psychobiology, Prentice-Hall, Englewood Cliffs, New Jersey, 1971.

[21] D.E. Berlyne, Exploration and curiosity. Science 153:25–33, 1966.

[22] S. Marsland, U. Nehmzow and J. Shapiro, A real-time novelty detector for a mobile robot, EUREL European Advanced Robotics Systems Masterclass and Conference, 2000.

[23] J.A. Easterbrook, The effect of emotion on cue utilization and the organisation of behavior. Psychological Review 66:183–201, 1959.

[24] D. Sperber and D. Wilson, Relevance: communication and cognition, Blackwell Publishing, Oxford, 1995.

[25] L. Fonar and P. Maes, Paying attention to what's important: using focus of attention to improve unsupervised learning, The Third International Conference on the Simulation of Adaptive Behavior (SAB94), Brighton, England, 1994.

[26] J.C. Stanley, Computer simulation of a model of habituation. Nature 26:146–148, 1976.

[27] T. Kohonen, Self-organization and associative memory, Springer, Berlin, 1993.

[28] R. Saunders and J.S. Gero, Curious agents and situated design evaluations. In: J.S. Gero and F.M.T. Brazier (Eds.), Agents in Design, Key Centre of Design Computing and Cognition, University of Sydney, pp. 133–149, 2002.

[29] R. Saunders and J.S. Gero, Situated design simulations using curious agents. AIEDAM 18(2):153–161, 2004.

[30] D. Helbing and P. Molnar, Social force model for pedestrian dynamics. Physical Review E 51:4282–4286, 1995.

[31] R. Saunders and J.S. Gero, Designing for interest and novelty: motivating design agents, CAAD Futures 2001, Kluwer, Dordrecht, pp. 725–738, 2001.

[32] J. Schmidhuber, A possibility for implementing curiosity and boredom in model-building neural controllers. In: J.A. Meyer and S.W. Wilson (Eds.), The International Conference on Simulation of Adaptive Behavior: From Animals to Animats, MIT Press/Bradford Books, pp. 222–227, 1991.

[33] D. Lenat, AM: An artificial intelligence approach to discovery in mathematics, Computer Science, Stanford University, 1976.

[34] J. Schmidhuber, What's interesting, Technical Report, Lugano, Switzerland, 1997.

[35] P.-Y. Oudeyer and F. Kaplan, Intelligent adaptive curiosity: a source of self-development, Fourth International Workshop on Epigenetic Robotics, Lund University, pp. 127–130, 2004.

[36] P.-Y. Oudeyer, F. Kaplan and V. Hafner, Intrinsic motivation systems for autonomous mental development. IEEE Transactions on Evolutionary Computation 11(2):265–286, 2007.

[37] F. Kaplan and P.-Y. Oudeyer, Motivational principles for visual know-how development. In: C.G. Prince, L. Berthouze, H. Kozima, D. Bullock, G. Stojanov and C. Balkenius (Eds.), Proceedings of the 3rd international workshop on Epigenetic Robotics: Modelling cognitive development in robotic systems, Lund University Cognitive Studies, pp. 73–80, 2003.

[38] E.C. Tolman, Purposive behavior in animals and men, Century, New York, 1932.

[39] B.F. Skinner, Behavior of organisms, Appleton-Century-Crofts, New York, 1938.

[40] J.W. Atkinson and N.T. Feather, A theory of achievement motivation, John Wiley, New York, 1966.

[41] J.W. Atkinson and J.O. Raynor, Motivation and achievement, V. H. Winston, Washington D. C, 1974.

[42] J.O. Raynor, Future orientation and motivation of immediate activity: an elaboration of the theory of achievement motivation. Psychological Review 76:606–610, 1969.

[43] F. Heider, The psychology of interpersonal relations, Wiley, New York, 1958.

[44] R.W. White, Motivation reconsidered: The concept of competence. Psychological Review 66:297–333, 1959.

[45] E. Deci and R. Ryan, Intrinsic motivation and self-determination in human behavior, Plenum Press, New York, 1985.

[46] J.M. Hunt, Implications of sequential order and hierarchy in early psychological development. Exceptional Infant 3, 1975.

[47] S. Singh, A.G. Barto and N. Chentanez, Intrinsically motivated reinforcement learning, Advances in Neural Information Processing Systems (NIPS) 17:1281–1288, 2005.

[48] D. Precup, R. Sutton and S. Singh, Theoretical results on reinforcement learning with temporally abstract options, The 10th European Conference on Machine Learning, Chemnitz, Germany, Springer Verlag, pp. 382–393, 1998.

[49] M. Csikszentmihalyi, Creativity: Flow and the psychology of discovery and invention, HarperCollins Publisher, New York, 1996.

[50] R. Saunders and J.S. Gero, The digital clockwork muse: a computational model of aesthetic evolution, The AISB'01 Symposium on Artificial Intelligence and Creativity in Arts and Science, SSAISB, 2001.

[51] C. Darwin, The origin of the species, John Murray, London, 1859.

[52] R.V. Gusarev, M.S. Burtsev and V.G. Red'ko, Alife model of evolutionary emergence of purposeful adaptive behavior, European Conference on Artificial Life, 2001.

[53] R. Stagner, Homeostasis, discrepancy, dissonance: a theory of motives and motivation. Motivation and Emotion 1:103–138, 1977.

[54] R.A. Brooks, How to build complete creatures rather than isolated cognitive simulators. In: K. VanLehn (Ed.), Architectures for Intelligence, Lawrence Erlbaum Associates, New Jersey, pp. 225–239, 1991.

Chapter 3
Towards Motivated Reinforcement Learning

Imbuing artificial agents with the ability to learn allows them to change their structure and improve their performance at a task [1]. Learning agents have the potential to make computer games more interesting because they can adapt in ways that reflexive agents cannot. Supervised learning, for example, has been used for behavioural cloning of players in multiuser games. The supervised learning agent observes a player's actions and learns to represent the player's avatar when the player is not online. Reinforcement learning [2] has been used to create non-player characters that can adapt their behaviour for specific tasks – such as fighting – in response to their opponent's behaviour during game play [3]. The focus of this book, motivated reinforcement learning, allows a new kind of non-player character that can not only adapt its behaviour for individual tasks, but also autonomously select which tasks to learn and do.

This chapter introduces the reinforcement learning framework in the context of non-player characters that can learn behaviour from their experiences interacting with their environment. The basics of the main variants of reinforcement learning are described, including the standard model, reinforcement learning for partially observable environments, function approximation for reinforcement learning, hierarchical reinforcement learning [4] and motivated reinforcement learning.

3.1 Defining Reinforcement Learning

Reinforcement learning (RL) is "learning what to do by trial-and-error". RL agents learn how to map situations to actions so as to maximise a numerical reward signal. The mapping they learn of situations (or states) to actions is called a behavioural policy. Formally, RL can be thought of as a computational reasoning process that, at each time step t, takes as input some representation $S_{(t)}$ of the sensed state of an environment and a reward value $R_{(t)}$ representing the value of that state. The RL process uses $S_{(t)}$ and $R_{(t)}$ to update a behavioural

K.E. Merrick, M.L. Maher, *Motivated Reinforcement Learning*, DOI 10.1007/978-3-540-89187-1_3,
© Springer-Verlag Berlin Heidelberg 2009

policy π and uses π to select an action $A_{(t)}$. A diagrammatic representation of the RL process is shown in Fig. 3.1.

As a concrete example of RL, consider the problem of a non-player character (NPC) monster that is repeatedly spawned to attack a castle. The monster is spawned in a world with states represented by a grid of locations and four movement actions for transitioning from one state to another in different directions. Prior to the monster interacting with the world, it is programmed with a reward signal that values transitions to the 'castle state' at 1 and all other transitions as 0, as shown in Fig. 3.2.

The monster is initially spawned at a random location. It interacts with the world using random trial-and-error to attempt to find the castle. The castle state is defined to be a terminal state. Each time the monster reaches the castle it receives a numerical reward of 1 and updates its policy to assign a percentage of this reward to each of the actions it took to successfully reach the castle. The monster is then respawned at, or reset to, a new, random location. After a number of such learning episodes, the monster's learned policy will include entries for the optimal action to take to achieve the castle state from any other state in the world.

This example illustrates how the reward signal focuses the RL on a specific task, attacking the castle. In addition, learning is episodic, requiring a reset (or respawn) between learning episodes. The remainder of this chapter studies variants of RL that modify these requirements, leading to motivated reinforcement learning (MRL) that uses a dynamic reward signal and permits continuous, adaptive learning.

Methods for learning the policy π fall into three fundamental classes: dynamic programming, Monte Carlo methods and temporal difference learning. These methods define update rules for learning approximations of π and action selection rules for using π to trigger action.

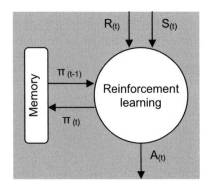

Fig. 3.1 The reinforcement learning process takes states and rewards as input, updates a policy stored in memory and outputs an action.

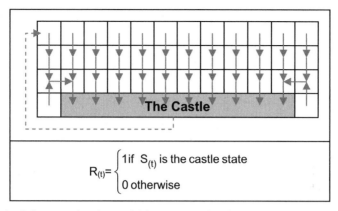

$$R_{(t)} = \begin{cases} 1 \text{ if } S_{(t)} \text{ is the castle state} \\ 0 \text{ otherwise} \end{cases}$$

Fig. 3.2 A reinforcement learning model for a monster learning to attack a castle. The reward signal (bottom) directs learning of a policy (top) for every state. The dotted arrow represents the resets that occur between learning episodes.

3.1.1 Dynamic Programming

Dynamic programming refers to a collection of algorithms used to compute optimal policies given a perfect model of an environment as a Markov Decision Process (MDP). A MDP consists of:

- a set **S** of sensed states;
- a set **A** of actions;
- a reward function $\mathcal{R}$: **S** x **A** → {Reals};
- a transition function $\mathcal{P}$: **S** x **A** → Π(**S**).

Two common strategies for learning an optimal policy π^* are to approximate the optimal value function $\mathcal{V}^*$ or the optimal action-value function Q^*. The optimal value function maps each observed state of the environment to the maximum expected return that can be achieved by starting in that state and always choosing the best actions. When knowledge of both the optimal value function and the probable consequences of each action in each state are available, an agent can choose an optimal policy. When the consequences of each action are not known, a strategy that approximates the optimal action-value function can be used. Such strategies map each sensed state and action to the maximum expected return starting from the given state and assuming that the specified action is taken and optimal actions chosen thereafter. Both $\mathcal{V}^*$ and Q^* can be defined using Bellman equations as follows:

$$V^*(S_{(t)}) = \max_{A_{(t)} \in A} \left[R(S_{(t)}, A_{(t)}) + \gamma \sum_{S_{(t+1)} \in S} P(S_{(t+1)} \mid S_{(t)}, A_{(t)}) \; V^*(S_{(t+1)}) \right]$$

$$Q^*(S_{(t)}, A_{(t)}) = R(S_{(t)}, A_{(t)}) + \gamma \sum_{S_{(t+1)} \in S} P(S_{(t+1)} \mid S_{(t)}, A_{(t)}) \max_{A_{(t+1)} \in A} Q^*(S_{(t+1)}, A_{(t+1)})$$

$P(S_{(t+1)} \mid S_{(t)}, A_{(t)})$ is the probability of making a transition $T_{(t+1)}$ from $S_{(t)}$ to $S_{(t+1)}$ when $A_{(t)}$ is chosen. $R(S_{(t)}, A_{(t)})$ is the expected reward for the same transition. The model is Markovian if the state transitions are independent of any previous sensed states or actions. General MDPs may have infinite state or action spaces; however a majority of RL approaches are designed to solve finite-state and finite-action problems. Dynamic programming algorithms are obtained by converting the Bellman equations into assignments, that is, update rules for improving approximations of the value function or action-value function. A detailed survey of dynamic programming techniques can be found in Chap. 4 of *Reinforcement Learning: An Introduction* [2].

Dynamic programming methods are well-developed mathematically and provide much of the theoretical foundation for RL. However, the requirement for a complete and accurate model of the environment in order for learning to occur renders them inappropriate in many complex or unpredictable environments such as virtual worlds. Monte Carlo methods and temporal difference learning extend RL to tasks where a full model is not available.

3.1.2   Monte Carlo Methods

Monte Carlo methods for RL require only experiences – in the form of sample sequences of states, actions and rewards – to facilitate learning. Monte Carlo methods assume that experiences are divided into episodes, each of which eventually terminate. Value estimates and policies are updated on completion of each episode. Most of the key ideas from dynamic programming have parallels in the Monte Carlo case. A detailed survey of Monte Carlo techniques can also be found in *Reinforcement Learning: An Introduction* [2], in Chap. 5.

While Monte Carlo methods are incremental in an episode-by-episode sense, they are not suited for step-by-step, incremental computation. In order to create NPCs capable of continuous, lifelong learning without episodic resets temporal difference learning methods are required.

3.1.3   Temporal Difference Learning

Temporal difference learning methods, like Monte Carlo methods, can learn directly from experience without a model of an environment's dynamics, however they are fully incremental and can learn at each step of interaction with an environment. This book uses Q-learning [5] as an example of a temporal difference learning method. A survey of other temporal difference methods can be found in Chap. 6 of *Reinforcement Learning: An Introduction* [2]. The update rule for Q-learning, which defines how Q is modified at each time-step, is:

$$Q(S_{(t)}, A_{(t)}) \leftarrow Q(S_{(t)}, A_{(t)}) + \beta[R_{(t)} + \gamma \max_{A_{(t+1)} \in A} Q(S_{(t+1)}, A_{(t+1)}) - Q(S_{(t)}, A_{(t)})]$$

where $\beta \in (0, 1]$ is a step-size parameter that controls how quickly Q changes at each update or backup and γ is the discount factor for expected future reward. The action to perform at each time step t is defined by an action selection rule. Typical action selection rules include ε-greedy or Boltzmann action selection that combine an exploration function f, such as random action selection, with greedy action selection as follows:

$$A_{(t+1)} = \arg \max_{A_{(t+1)} \in A} f(Q(S_{(t+1)}, A_{(t+1)}))$$

While the RL framework does not stipulate any properties for the reward signal $R_{(t)}$, other than that it is a simple real number, in practice, reward is typically defined using a rule-based representation that comprises a set of conditions about subsets of the state space or transition space and numerical values for states or transitions in those subsets. This representation is shown below:

$$R_{(t)} = \begin{cases} R_1 \text{ if } S_{(t)} \in \mathbf{S}_1 \\ R_2 \text{ if } S_{(t)} \in \mathbf{S}_2 \\ ... \\ R_r \text{ if } T_{(t)} \in \mathbf{T}_1 \\ R_{r+1} \text{ if } T_{(t)} \in \mathbf{T}_2 \\ ... \\ R_R \quad \text{otherwise} \end{cases}$$

The subsets $\mathbf{S}_1$, $\mathbf{S}_2$, ... and $\mathbf{T}_1$, $\mathbf{T}_2$, ... generally describe states or transitions of particularly high or low value with respect to some task. R_R is often zero or a small action penalty. An example of a rule-based reward signal was shown for the castle attacking task in Fig. 3.2.

Using a rule-based representation for reward signals, a change in the state space that renders all subsets $\mathbf{S}_r$ and $\mathbf{T}_r$ for which $R_r \neq R_R$ impossible to achieve, will cause the learned behaviour to degenerate to the exploration function, which is often random action selection. Likewise, states or transitions that are not elements of any subset $\mathbf{S}_r$ or $\mathbf{T}_r$ for which a reward value has been defined will not influence the learned behaviour of the agent, other than as a means for achieving states or transitions for which a higher reward value has been defined. This form of reward signal limits RL to environments in which such changes will not occur for the duration of the learning agent's lifetime and to environments where it is possible to value subsets $\mathbf{S}_1$, $\mathbf{S}_2$, ... and $\mathbf{T}_1$, $\mathbf{T}_2$, ... offline, before learning begins. In dynamic virtual worlds where tasks may only be relevant for short periods and new tasks may arise, it may be difficult to predict which tasks to learn without first interacting with the environment. This makes the definition of a fixed, task-oriented reward signal or start and terminal states problematic prior to interaction with the world. As an alternative, MRL uses a motivation signal generated while learning is in progress based on the agent's experiences in its environment as a key element of attention focus for RL. This is discussed further in Sect. 3.3.

Previously, agent experiences have been modelled in one of two ways: episodic or continuing task experiences. Episodic experiences are modelled as one or more finite full-trajectories of states, actions and rewards:

$$S_{(t)}, A_{(t)}, R_{(t)}, S_{(t+1)}, A_{(t+1)}, R_{(t+1)}, \ldots S_{(t+N)}, A_{(t+N)}, R_{(t+N)}$$

where a full-trajectory can be decomposed into a state trajectory $S_{(t)}$, $S_{(t+1)}$, $S_{(t+2)}$ ... $S_{(t+N)}$, action trajectory $A_{(t)}$, $A_{(t+1)}$, $A_{(t+2)}$ ... $A_{(t+N)}$ and reward trajectory $R_{(t)}$, $R_{(t+1)}$, $R_{(t+2)}$ ... $R_{(t+N)}$. Continuing task experiences have the same constituent trajectories. However, continuing task experiences are represented by a single, infinite full-trajectory of states, actions and rewards:

$$S_{(t)}, A_{(t)}, R_{(t)}, S_{(t+1)}, A_{(t+1)}, R_{(t+1)}, S_{(t+2)}, A_{(t+2)}, R_{(t+2)}, \ldots$$

The basic RL process for learning policies for rewarded tasks uses generalised policy iteration (GPI). GPI describes the interaction between policy evaluation, such as the Q-learning update, and policy improvement such as the Q-learning action selection rule. Policy improvement makes the policy greedy with respect to the current value function while policy evaluation brings the value function closer to the current policy. The most common flow of control for RL algorithms assumes episodic experiences. The learning agent is reset each time some predefined terminal state is reached, often states in which very high or very low reward is achieved. The time between resets is referred to as a learning episode as shown in the algorithm in Fig. 3.3.

The reset may move the learning agent to a random position in the state space or to some predefined start state. This encourages the learned policy to form a mapping from every state in the environment to an action. The reset operation does not have to be part of the world model as is the case in the castle attacking task described above.

```
Initialise Q(S, A) arbitrarily
Repeat (for each episode):
    Reset S(t)
    Repeat (until S(t) is terminal):
        Choose A(t) from S(t) using the policy improvement fn
        Execute A(t)
        Sense R(t+1) and S(t+1)
        Update π using the policy evaluation function
        S(t) ← S(t+1)
```

Fig. 3.3 Episodic temporal difference reinforcement learning algorithms process experiences in distinct episodes.

While an episodic flow of control is sufficient for learning single, episodic tasks – such as monster spawning to attack a castle – for other NPCs continuous, lifelong learning is an advantage. One example of an NPC in the latter category is a bartender. The bartender needs to perform different tasks at different times, such as opening the bar, serving customers, cleaning tables, and closing the bar. The behaviour of the bartender needs to form a continuous cycle in which different tasks are performed at different times. To achieve such behavioural cycles, non-episodic learning without resets is required. Some work has been done with continuing task RL algorithms – such as the R-learning algorithm for undiscounted continuing tasks. In addition, many episodic RL approaches can be adapted to the continuing task setting. A continuing task RL algorithm for discounted tasks is shown in Fig. 3.4. The MRL models described in this book use a continuing task approach to learning to create NPCs capable of continuous, lifelong learning of multiple tasks.

```
Initialise Q(S, A) arbitrarily
Initialise S(t)
Repeat (forever):
    Choose A(t) from S(t) using the policy improvement function
    Execute A(t)
    Sense R(t) and S(t+1)
    Update π using the policy evaluation function
    S(t) ← S(t+1)
```

Fig. 3.4 Continuing task, temporal difference reinforcement learning algorithms process experiences as a single, infinite trajectory.

3.2 Reinforcement Learning in Complex Environments

The algorithms described above assume a perfect model of the environment as a MDP. However many environments, including many virtual world scenarios, do not conform to this assumption. As a result, a range of RL variants have been developed to permit learning in different types of environments. This section introduces the basics of some of the more common variants and how they differ to MRL.

3.2.1   Partially Observable Environments

In RL, a state S may use an attribute-based representation that comprises a fixed-length vector of $|S|$ sensations $(s_1, s_2, \ldots , s_{|S|})$. This representation assumes that the learning process will only reason about a fixed set of sensations. Any attributes beyond those comprising S will not influence the learning process. When the sensations $s_1, s_2, \ldots s_{|S|}$ completely describe the actual world state W of an environment, the environment is said to be fully observable. When W contains attributes beyond those included in S the environment is partially observable. Partially observable environments can be modelled as partially observable Markov Decision Processes (POMDPs). A POMDP consists of:

- a set **W** of world states;

- a set **S** of sensed states;

- a set **A** of actions;

- a reward function $\mathcal{R}$: **W** x **A** x **W** $\rightarrow$ {Reals};

- a transition function $\mathcal{P}$: **W** x **A** x **S** $\rightarrow$ Π(**S**).

In partially observable environments $\mathcal{P}(W_{(t+1)}, S_{(t+1)} | W_{(t)}, A_{(t)})$ is the probability of making a transition $T_{(t+1)}$ from $W_{(t)}$ to $W_{(t+1)}$ and sensing $S_{(t+1)}$ when $A_{(t)}$ is chosen. $\mathcal{R}(W_{(t)}, A_{(t)}, W_{(t+1)})$ is the expected reward for the same transition. A diagrammatic representation of the RL process in a partially observable environment is shown in Fig. 3.5.

While a large body of work has focused on developing variants of RL for partially observable environments, these algorithms generally begin with the assumption that partial observability is a disadvantage. As such, algorithms for solving POMDPs focus on techniques for discovering hidden state information in order to learn optimal policies. In complex environments such as online virtual worlds, however, partial observability can be an advantage. The MRL models presented in Part II permit agents to focus attention by either deliberately sensing only part of the world state or deliberately observing only part of the sensed state. Limiting the sensations to which the learning agent responds enables agents to learn in complex environments by ignoring stimuli that are not relevant to their current behaviour.

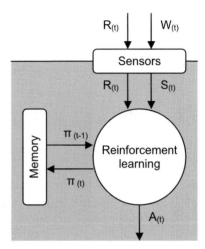

Fig. 3.5 The reinforcement learning process for partially observable environments. Sensed states differ from the actual world state.

3.2.2 Function Approximation

In fully or partially observable environments with small state spaces, such as the castle attacking world, it is feasible to represent the value function $\mathcal{V}$ or action-value function Q for the learned policy as a table, explicitly mapping states, actions and utility values. However, in large-scale virtual worlds the state space may be too large for such a representation to be feasible. Function approximation techniques extend RL to such environments by representing the value function or action-value function as a parameterised functional form with a parameter vector $\Theta_{(t)}$. In value prediction with function approximation the value function $\mathcal{V}$ is dependent on $\Theta_{(t)}$ and varies from time-step to time-step only as $\Theta_{(t)}$ varies. $\mathcal{V}$ might be the function computed by an artificial neural network with $\Theta_{(t)}$ the vector of connection weights or the function computed by a decision tree where $\Theta_{(t)}$ is the vector of parameters defining the split points and leaf values of the tree. In action-value prediction with function approximation Q might be computed using gradient-descent methods. Typically, the number of parameters in $\Theta_{(t)}$ is much less than the number of states so changing one parameter changes the estimated value of many states. This generalisation over the state space reduces the memory requirements of RL in environments with large or continuous value state spaces.

While a large body of research has focused on the development of function approximation techniques for RL, this work continues to assume that the reward signal uses rules about states or transitions to represent a single task for which a single solution policy should be learned. In the context of NPCs, this means that each character can only solve a single task represented by the reward signal. In contrast MRL models assume that learning tasks may be situated in a wider environment made complex by the presence of multiple-tasks that may change over time. This permits the design of NPCs that can adapt their behaviour to multiple tasks as required at different times.

3.2.3 Hierarchical Reinforcement Learning

Hierarchical reinforcement learning (HRL) recognises that complex environments may contain repeatable substructures and attempts to improve the scalability of RL in structured environments by creating temporal abstractions of repeated structures in the state space. Temporal abstractions encapsulate behaviours that can be recalled and reused during learning. Using temporal abstractions, decisions are not required at each step but rather the execution of temporally extended behaviours is invoked. These behaviours follow their own policies until termination, leading naturally to hierarchical control architectures and learning algorithms.

HRL extends RL by the addition of a set **B** of behavioural options [6] or similar data structures that represent the solutions to subtasks of the task defined by the reward signal. Over time, the agent identifies and learns behaviours represented by options. These then become available to the agent as action choices resulting in the development of hierarchical collections of behaviours. HRL can be thought of as a reasoning process that, at each time step t, takes as input some representation $S_{(t)}$ of the sensed state of an environment and a reward value $R_{(t)}$ representing the value of that state. The HRL process uses $S_{(t)}$ and $R_{(t)}$ to modify a set **B** of behaviours and to modify a behavioural policy π and uses π to output an action $A_{(t)}$. A diagrammatic representation of the HRL process is shown in Fig. 3.6.

In the MDP formulation for RL, only the sequential nature of the decision process is relevant, not the amount of time that passes between decision stages. A generalisation of this is the Semi-Markov Decision Process (SMDP) in which the amount of time between one decision and the next is a real or integer valued random variable. In the integer value case, SMDPs model discrete-time, discrete-event systems. In such systems, decisions can be made at positive integer multiples of an underlying time-step. The discrete-time SMDP formulation underlies most approaches to HRL.

Fig. 3.6 The hierarchical
reinforcement learning process
takes states and rewards as input,
creates behavioural options,
updates a hierarchical policy
stored in memory and outputs an
action.

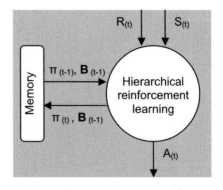

The Bellman equations for $\mathcal{V}^*$ and Q^* can be modified to model SMDPs by incorporating a random variable τ that denotes the waiting time in the sensed state $S_{(t)}$ when the action $A_{(t)}$ is executed.

$$\mathcal{V}^*(S_{(t)}) = \max_{A_{(t)} \in \mathbf{A}} \left[\mathcal{R}_{\cdot}(S_{(t)}, A_{(t)}) + \sum_{S_{(t+\tau)} \in \mathbf{S}, \tau} \gamma^\tau \, \mathcal{P}(S_{(t+\tau)}, \tau \mid S_{(t)}, A_{(t)}) \, \mathcal{V}^*(S_{(t+\tau)}) \right]$$

$$Q^*(S_{(t)}, A_{(t)}) = \mathcal{R}(S_{(t)}, A_{(t)}) + \sum_{S_{(t+\tau)} \in \mathbf{S}, \tau} \gamma^\tau \, \mathcal{P}(S_{(t+\tau)}, \tau \mid S_{(t)}, A_{(t)}) \max_{A_{(t+\tau)} \in \mathbf{A}} Q^*(S_{(t+\tau)}, A_{(t+\tau)})$$

The transition probabilities generalise to give the joint probability that a transition from state $S_{(t)}$ to state $S_{(t+\tau)}$ occurs after τ time-steps when the action $A_{(t)}$ is executed. This joint probability is written as $\mathcal{P}(S_{(t+\tau)}, \tau \mid S_{(t)}, A_{(t)})$. The expected immediate rewards $\mathcal{R}(S_{(t)}, A_{(t)})$ now give the amount of discounted reward expected to accumulate over the waiting time in $S_{(t)}$ given action $A_{(t)}$ is executed.

Q-learning can be applied to SMDPs by interpreting the immediate reward $R_{(t)}$ as the return accumulated during the waiting time in state $S_{(t)}$ and adjusting the discounting to reflect the waiting time. In the hierarchical case, the update rule for Q-learning becomes:

$$Q(S_{(t)}, A_{(t)}) \leftarrow Q(S_{(t)}, A_{(t)}) + \beta[R_{(t)} + \gamma^\tau \max_{A_{(t+\tau)} \in \mathbf{A}} Q(S_{(t+\tau)}, A_{(t+\tau)}) - Q(S_{(t)}, A_{(t)})]$$

where $R_{(t)} = R_{(t+1)} + \gamma R_{(t+2)} + \dots + \gamma^{\tau-1} R_{(t+\tau)}$. The return accumulated during the waiting time must be bounded and can be computed recursively during the waiting time. Bradtke and Duff [7] showed how to do this for continuous-time SMDPs and Parr [8] proved that it converges under essentially the same conditions required for Q-learning convergence.

In order to establish a theory for behavioural policies that are a hierarchical collection of actions and other policies, Precup [6] introduced the notion of temporal abstractions called options. An 'option' is a behaviour that is initiated, takes control for some period of time and then eventually ends. An option $B = \langle \mathbf{I}, \pi, \Omega \rangle$ comprises an initiation set of states $\mathbf{I}$ in which the option applies, an option policy π that specifies what actions are executed by the option for a subset of environment states and a termination function Ω that specifies the conditions under which the option terminates. The termination condition $\Omega(S_{(t)}) \rightarrow [0, 1]$ defines the probability with which the option will terminate in the state $S_{(t)}$. Options can invoke other options as actions, thus making it possible for behaviours to have a hierarchical structure.

In order to treat options as much as possible as if they are conventional single-step actions, Sutton et al. [9] introduced the concept of a multi-time model of an option that generalises the single-step model. In their multi-time model, $\mathcal{P}(S_{(t+\tau)} \mid S_{(t)}, B_{(t)})$ is a combination of the probability that $S_{(t+\tau)}$ is the state in which the option $B_{(t)}$ terminates, together with a measure of how delayed that outcome is in terms of γ:

$$\mathcal{P}(S_{(t+\tau)} \mid S_{(t)}, B_{(t)}) = \sum_{\tau=1}^{\infty} \mathcal{P}(S_{(t+\tau)}, \tau)\, \gamma^{\tau}$$

$\mathcal{R}(S_{(t)}, B_{(t)})$ is the expected cumulative reward for the same transition. These generalisations can be used to define generalised forms of the Bellman optimality equations for $\mathcal{V}^*$ and Q^*. These generalised forms reduce to the usual Bellman optimality equations if all the options are one-step options (primitive actions).

$$\mathcal{V}^*(S_{(t)}) = \max_{B_{(t)} \in \mathbf{B}} \left[\mathcal{R}(S_{(t)}, B_{(t)}) + \sum_{S_{(t+\tau)} \in \mathbf{S}} \mathcal{P}(S_{(t+\tau)} \mid S_{(t)}, B_{(t)})\, \mathcal{V}^*(S_{(t+\tau)}) \right]$$

$$Q^*(S_{(t)}, B_{(t)}) = \mathcal{R}(S_{(t)}, B_{(t)}) + \sum_{S_{(t+\tau)} \in \mathbf{S}} \mathcal{P}(S_{(t+\tau)} \mid S_{(t)}, B_{(t)}) \max_{B_{(t+\tau)} \in \mathbf{B}} Q^*(S_{(t+\tau)}, B_{(t+\tau)})$$

The corresponding Q-learning update is:

$$Q(S_{(t)}, B_{(t)}) \leftarrow Q(S_{(t)}, B_{(t)}) + \beta[R_{(t)} + \gamma^{\tau} \max_{B_{(t+\tau)} \in \mathbf{B}} Q(S_{(t+\tau)}, B_{(t+\tau)}) - Q(S_{(t)}, B_{(t)})]$$

where $R_{(t)}$ is the reward accumulated during the execution of option $B_{(t)}$. The optimal behaviour to perform at each time step is defined by the behaviour selection rule:

$$B_{(t+\tau)} = \underset{B_{(t+\tau)} \in \mathbf{B}}{\arg\max} \; f(Q(S_{(t+\tau)}, B_{(t+\tau)}))$$

A discussion of other approaches to formalising HRL can be found in the survey paper by Barto and Mahadevan [4].

HRL recognises that many environments contain repeatable substructures that can be abstracted as reusable behavioural options. However, HRL, like function approximation, assumes the presence of a reward signal that uses rules about states or transitions to represents a single task for which a single solution policy should be learned. This single solution policy is represented by the root policy in the policy hierarchy. Furthermore, existing HRL techniques assume that learning will be episodic. MRL draws on the idea that many environments contain repeatable substructures but rejects the notion that these must represent subtasks of a single root task. MRL assumes that substructures in the state space may represent independent MDPs. The role of motivation in RL is thus to identify and focus on these substructures.

HRL techniques can be thought of as a precursor to MRL and particularly motivated hierarchical reinforcement learning (MHRL) in that they introduce the idea of using task-independent rules to identify substructures within a given state space. McGovern [10], for example, used the idea of bottleneck states traversed frequently in successful learning episodes to initiate learning of behavioural options for HRL. Hengst [11] developed a more flexible model in which substructure identification depends on the frequency of variable changes within the state space. His model no longer relies on the reward signal to identify substructures, meaning that the HRL agent can identify and solve subtasks of tasks for which high values of the reward signal only occurs after a long period of time. Simsek and Barto [12] developed a similar model using relative novelty as the means of identifying substructures independently of the reward signal. However, McGovern's [10] model assumes episodic learning and both the Hengst [11] and Simsek [12] models assume a period of offline exploration to identify substructures in the state space before the learning phase begins. In contrast, MHRL models attempt to formalise the identification of substructures in the state space as a motivation process that can compute motivation values from experiences, while learning is in progress.

3.3 Motivated Reinforcement Learning

A number of different models exist for MRL that have been designed to extend RL in a range of different ways. MRL models can be considered in two broad categories: category (I) models that introduce a motivation signal in addition to the reward signal; and category (II) models that use the motivation signal instead of the reward signal. Within these categories, MRL models can also be characterised by the type of RL algorithm they incorporate. Existing work has focused on incorporating motivation with RL and HRL algorithms although the use of motivation with other algorithms such as function approximation methods is also conceivable. The purpose of the models within these categories has also been varied. Some MRL models are designed to speed RL and have similar goals to HRL. Other models are designed to achieve more adaptive or multitask learning through the use of motivation as an automatic attention focus mechanism.

The term motivation signal is used here to distinguish a type of reward signal that is computed online as a function of an agent's experiences using a computational model of motivation, rather than as a set of predefined rules mapping values to known environmental states or transitions. Category (I) models such as those shown in Fig. 3.7, incorporate a motivation signal $R_{m(t)}$ in addition to a reward signal $R_{(t)}$. Models in this category have focused on the use of motivation primarily in RL and HRL settings. The purpose of these models has been to speed up existing RL algorithms by the addition of a motivation signal, but also to achieve more adaptive, multitask learning by using motivation as an automatic attention focus mechanism. MHRL models in this category formalise the process of identifying subtasks as a motivation process that produces a motivation signal $R_{m(t)}$ in addition to the standard reward signal $R_{(t)}$ from the environment. The primary purpose of the motivation signal is to direct learning by identifying subtasks of the task defined by the reward signal. These models adhere most closely to the goals of RL and HRL, aiming to speed the learning of the rewarded task.

The second broad category of MRL models incorporates a motivation signal $R_{m(t)}$ instead of, rather than in addition to, the reward signal as shown in Fig. 3.8. This approach has been used primarily in conjunction with RL algorithms. While a number of HRL and MHRL(I) models claim to extend to the MHRL(II) scenario, there are few empirical results describing such models.

3.3.1 Using a Motivation Signal in Addition to a Reward Signal

MRL(I) models incorporate both a reward signal from the environment and a motivation signal with RL as in Fig. 3.7(a). A motivation process reasons about the current sensed state $S_{(t)}$ and some representation of the set **S** of all sensed states encountered so far, to produce a motivation signal $R_{m(t)}$. This motivation signal is then combined with the reward signal $R_{(t)}$ according to some rule or weighting and the combined value used as input for an RL process such as Q-learning.

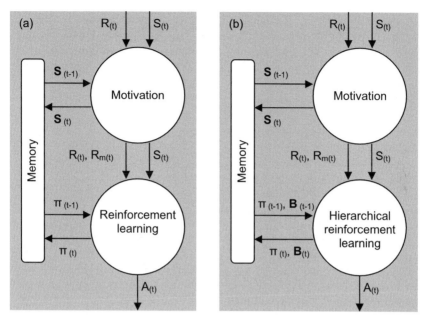

Fig. 3.7 Category (I) motivated reinforcement learning models: **(a)** MRL(I) and **(b)** MHRL(I) extend reinforcement learning and hierarchical reinforcement learning by introducing a motivation signal in addition to the reward signal.

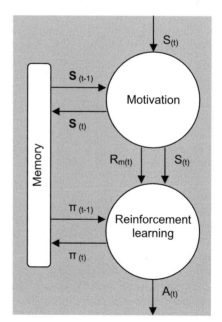

Fig. 3.8 Category (II) motivated reinforcement learning models extend reinforcement learning by using a motivation signal instead of the reward signal.

   Huang and Weng [13] implemented a MRL(I) model in order to develop a robotic value system for use with a simple machine vision system. In their model the motivation signal is defined using a computational model of novelty. Novelty is based on the level of agreement between expected sensations and actual sensations. Each time a state $S_{(t)} = (s_{1(t)}, s_{2(t)}, \dots s_{|S|(t)})$ is sensed, the novelty $N_{(t)}$ of the state is measured as the difference between primed sensations $s'_{i(t)}$ and actual sensations $s_{i(t+1)}$ as follows:

$$N_{(t)} = \sqrt{\frac{1}{|S|} \sum_{i=1}^{|S|} \frac{(s'_{i(t)} - s_{i(t+1)})^2}{\sigma_i^2}}$$

A primed sensation is a prediction about what will be sensed after a certain action is taken. Primed sensations are computed using an Incremental Hierarchical Discriminant Regression (IHDR) [14] tree that derives the most discriminating features from sensed states in the set **S**. σ_i is the expected deviation that is calculated as the time-discounted average of the squared difference $(s'_{i(t)} - s_{i(t+1)})^2$. The more accurately the robot can predict what will happen in the next state, the lower the novelty.

   In addition to the motivation signal, Huang and Weng [13] incorporate a reward signal from a human teacher in the environment. Reward is fed to the agent using two buttons for 'good' and 'bad' controlled by the teacher. The reward and motivation signals are combined as a weighted sum:

$$\{ R_{m(t)}, R_{(t)} \} = \alpha \mathcal{F}^+ + \beta \mathcal{F}^- + (1 - \alpha - \beta) N_{(t)}$$

where $0 < \alpha$ and $\beta < 1$ are parameters indicating the relative weight between the positive component $\mathcal{F}^+$ of $R_{(t)}$, the negative component $\mathcal{F}^-$ of $R_{(t)}$ and the motivation signal, novelty $N_{(t)}$. The combined value is then passed to the learning process.

   In general, novelty-based models of motivation can become problematic in environments that may contain random occurrences, as is the case in many real-world domains. According to the model developed by Huang and Weng [13], for example, primed sensations will almost always differ from actual sensations in the case of a random occurrence. This means that random occurrences will tend to be highly novel. In their simplified experiments with robotic vision, Huang and Weng [13] used a random flashing image to demonstrate how a SAIL robot using their model maintains its visual focus on highly novel occurrences. However, if a more complex and realistic world model is assumed, random occurrences are most likely to represent noise from the robot's sensors. In such domains, there is generally little to be learned from random occurrences. In addition, this model assumes the existence of a human teacher to direct the robot's learning through the provision of 'good' and 'bad' reward. The novelty based motivation function is viewed as an additional exploration function to supplement this learning. This book extends the role of motivation to that of the primary attention focus mechanism in RL, thus removing the need for a human teacher.

Other models of motivation in MRL(I) settings have focused on more complex cognitive phenomena such as interest, curiosity and boredom that avoid the problems of novelty-based models. Schmidhuber, one of the earliest researchers to experiment with MRL models, proposed several cognitive models of motivation. In his framework for Curious Neural Controllers, Schmidhuber [15] used the predictability of a learned world model to represent curiosity and boredom as reinforcement and pain units. Predictability P is measured as the result of classifying sequential sensations $s_{i(t)}$ and $s_{i(t+1)}$ using a self-supervised neural network to represent the set **S** of all sensed states:

$$P_{i(t+1)} = s_{i(t+1)}(1 - s_{i(t+1)})(\sum_n w_{in} \ P_{i(t)} + \delta_i s_{i(t)})$$

where w_{in} is the weight connecting neurons i and n. Schmidhuber's Curious Neural Controller is designed to identify states where the model network's prediction performance is not optimal as the most highly motivating, in order to encourage an agent to revisit those states and improve its network model. Zero motivation $R_{m(t)}$ is given in cases of maximum predictability and also in cases of very low predictability to simulate boredom in such states. Maximum motivation is generated for moderate levels of predictability to represent curiosity about states in which an "ideal mismatch" occurs between what is expected and what is sensed. This motivation process is designed to represent the theory that a system cannot learn something that it does not almost know already. The direct goal of curiosity and boredom in Schmidhuber's model is to improve the world model represented by the self-supervised neural network, while the indirect goal is to ease the learning of tasks defined by a reward signal. In later work, Schmidhuber shows empirically that use of a motivation signal can speed RL of rewarded tasks using a curious, creative explorer with two co-evolving brains as the motivation model [16]. He claims that his models may also be appropriate in settings without a reward signal. However he states that there is no way to evaluate the resulting agents.

Simsek and Barto [17] propose a different framework for MRL(I), shown in Fig. 3.9, which is designed to learn how to accumulate reward in the most efficient manner, without necessarily accumulating that reward. They refer to this as "optimal exploration" for the purpose of learning a policy that will enable exploitation when needed at a later time. In their framework, agents maintain two value functions: one that is used to represent the learned policy to a rewarded task and another that is used to select actions. These are called the 'task value function' and the 'behaviour value function', respectively. The task value function produces a motivation signal for directing the behaviour value function by observing the immediate reward and the state of the environment as follows:

$$R_{m(t)} = p + \sum_{S \in S} (V_{(t)}^{\max}(S) - V_{(t-1)}^{\max}(S)) \text{ where } V_{(t)}^{\max}(S) = \max_{T < t} V_{(T)}^{\max}(S)$$

$p < 0$ is a small action penalty. In the Simsek and Barto [17] model, the reward signal takes the form in the equation above and continues to use the assumption that the reward signal uses rules about states or transitions to represent a single task for which a single solution policy should be learned.

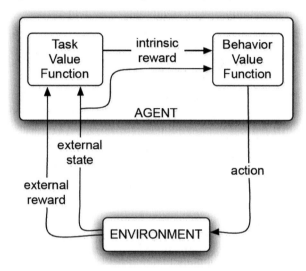

Fig. 3.9 Simsek and Barto [17] model MHRL(I) agents using a task value function and a behaviour value function.

MHRL(I) models extend MRL(I) models by incorporating the ability to recall and reuse learned behaviours. This can further improve learning efficiency when compared to MRL(I) or RL models. MHRL(I) models incorporate both a reward signal and a motivation signal with HRL as in Figure 3.7(a). Singh et al. [18] model MHRL by splitting the environment in which HRL is occurring into external and internal components as shown in Fig. 3.10. Stimuli from the external environment can be interpreted by the critic to produce an extrinsic reward signal. This extrinsic reward signal may be combined with internal reward (motivation) computed based on the internal environment.

Each first encounter with a salient event initiates the learning of an option and an option-model [6] for that event. A motivation signal is generated each time the event is encountered. The motivation signal is proportional to the

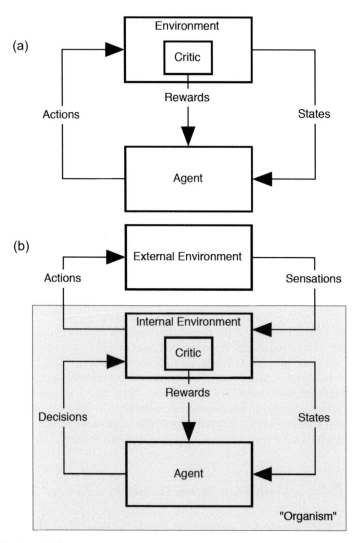

Fig. 3.10 (a) Reinforcement learning is extended by Barto et al. [19] by splitting the environment into internal and external components to create **(b)** category (I) motivated reinforcement learning agents.

error in the prediction of the event according to the learned option-model for that event. When the agent encounters an unpredicted salient event a few times, its updated action-value function drives it to repeatedly attempt to achieve that event. The agent acts on the environment according to an ε-greedy policy with respect to an action-value function that is learned using a mix of Q-learning and SMDP planning. As the agent moves around the world, all the options and their models initiated so far are simultaneously updated using intra-option learning algorithms. Initially, only the primitive actions in the environment are available to the agent. Over time, the agent identifies and learns behaviours represented by options and option-models. These then become available to the agent as action choices resulting in the development of hierarchical collections of behaviours. As the agent tries repeatedly to achieve salient events, learning improves both its policy for doing so and its option-model that predicts the event. As the option policy and option-model improve, the motivation signal diminishes and the agent becomes bored and moves on.

Singh et al. [18] model the motivation signal generated in response to a state $S_{(t)}$ that follows a salient event as proportional to the error in the prediction of the event, according to the learned option model B for the event. The motivation signal is zero otherwise, as shown below. The motivation signal and reward signal are combined as a sum in the Q-learning update of the behaviour action-value function.

$$R_{m(t)} = \begin{cases} \varphi[1 - P^B(S_{(t+1)} \mid S_{(t)})] & \text{if } S_{(t)} \text{ is a salient event} \\ 0 & \text{otherwise} \end{cases}$$

Thus, in this MHRL(I) model the motivation signal is used to assign a strength to a salient, motivating event. However, Singh et al. [18] do not focus on how salient events are identified. While they identify that their model is general enough to incorporate aspects of motivation such as internal state, memories and accumulated knowledge [19], in practice they use a simple rule-based model in which changes in light and sound intensity are salient events. This is used in conjunction with a reward signal that uses rules about states and transitions to reward a single task in a simple playroom domain.

3.3.2   Using a Motivation Signal Instead of a Reward Signal

MRL(II) models incorporate a motivation signal with RL instead of the reward signal from the environment as shown in Fig. 3.8. The motivation process reasons about the current sensed state $S_{(t)}$ and some representation of the set **S** of all sensed states encountered so far to produce a motivation signal $R_{m(t)}$ that is used as input for a RL algorithm such as Q-learning.

Saunders and Gero [20] experimented with a MRL(II) model that incorporates a computational model of novelty with RL in order to develop design agents capable of both problem finding and problem solving in complex design spaces. Problem finding is the process of identifying novel design tasks, while problem solving is the search for novel solutions to those tasks. In contrast to Huang and Weng [13], Saunders and Gero [20] use a Habituated

Self-Organising Map (HSOM) [21] rather than an IHDR tree to represent the set **S** of sensed states and model novelty. An HSOM consists of a standard Self-Organising Map (SOM) [22] with an additional habituating neuron connected to every clustering neuron of the SOM. A SOM consists of a topologically structured set **U** of neurons, each of which represents a cluster of sensed states. Each time a stimulus $S_{(t)} = (s_{1(t)}, s_{2(t)}, \ldots s_{|S|(t)})$ is presented to the SOM a winning neuron $U_{(t)} = (u_{1(t)}, u_{2(t)}, \ldots u_{|S|(t)})$ is chosen that best matches the stimulus. This is done by selecting the neuron with the minimum distance d to the stimulus where d is calculated as:

$$d = \sqrt{\sum_{i=1}^{|S|} (u_{i(t)} - s_{i(t)})^2}$$

The winning neuron and its eight topological neighbours are moved closer to the input stimulus by adjusting their weights according to:

$$u_{i(t+1)} = u_{i(t)} + \eta\,(s_{i(t)} - u_{i(t)})$$

where $0 \leq \eta \leq 1$ is the learning rate of the SOM. The neighbourhood size and learning rate are kept constant so the SOM is always learning. The activities of the winning neuron and its neighbours are propagated up the synapse to the habituating layer as a synaptic value $\varsigma_{(t)} = 1$. Neurons that do not belong to the winning neighbourhood give an input of $\varsigma_{(t)} = 0$ to the synapse. The synaptic efficacy, or novelty, $N_{(t)}$, is then calculated using Stanley's model of habituation [23]:

$$\tau\frac{dN_{(t)}}{dt} = \alpha\,[N_{(0)} - N_{(t)}] - \varsigma_{(t)}$$

$N_{(0)} = 1$ is the initial novelty value, τ is a constant governing the rate of habituation and α is a constant governing the rate of recovery. $N_{(t)}$ is calculated stepwise at time t by using the value $N_{(t-1)}$ stored in the habituating neuron to calculate the derivative from the equation above and then approximating $N_{(t)}$ as follows:

$$N_{(t)} = N_{(t-1)} + \frac{dN_{(t-1)}}{dt}$$

While this novelty-based model is particularly appropriate for design agents, it poses problems similar to those in the Huang and Weng [13] model when used in environments that may contain random occurrences. In such environments, alternatives to novelty-based techniques for modelling motivation are required.

Kaplan and Oudeyer [24] developed several alternatives that overcome the problems associated with novelty-based models by using an approach designed to motivate a search for situations that show the greatest potential for learning. In one such model, they define such situations in terms of three motivational variables: predictability, familiarity and stability of the sensory-motor context of a robot. The sensory-motor vector at time t is defined as comprising all possible sensations and actions: $SM_{(t)} = (s_{1(t)}, s_{2(t)}, \ldots s_{|S|(t)} \ldots, A_{1(t)}, A_{2(t)}, \ldots)$. Predictability $P_{(t)}$ is defined as the current error e for predicting the sensed state $S_{(t)}$ given the sensory-motor vector $SM_{(t-1)}$:

$$P_{(t)} = 1 - e(SM_{(t-1)}, S_{(t)})$$

Familiarity $\Gamma_{(t)}$ is a measure of how common the transition is between $SM_{(t-1)}$ and $S_{(t)}$. Familiarity is defined in terms of the frequency f of the sensory-motor transition for a recent period $t - \tau$.

$$\Gamma_{(t)} = f_\tau(SM_{(t-1)}, S_{(t)})$$

Finally, stability $\sigma_{i(t)}$ measures the distance of an observation $s_{i(t)}$ in the sensed state $S_{(t)}$ from its average value $s_{i(\tau)}$ in a recent period $t - \tau$. Each robotic agent is motivated by multiple stability variables, each associated with a specific joint or domain feature for which the robot is to be motivated to maintain stability. For example, Kaplan and Oudeyer [24] used four stability variables for the head and neck joints called 'head pan position', 'head tilt position', 'relative light pan position' and 'relative light tilt position'. The resulting agent is motivated to maintain the stability of its head position relative to a light source.

$$\sigma_{i(t)} = 1 - \sqrt{\left(s_{i(t)} - s_{i(\tau)}\right)^2}$$

The motivation signal is constructed from the equations for predictability, familiarity and stability using the intuition that reward should be highest when stability is maximised and when predictability and familiarity are increasing. Increasing predictability and familiarity precludes highly novel stimuli like random occurrences from becoming highly motivating unless they become more predictable and familiar and thus less random.

$$R_{m(t)} = \sigma_{1(t)} + \sigma_{2(t)} + \ldots +$$
$$\begin{cases} \Gamma_{(t)} - \Gamma_{(t-1)} : \Gamma_{(t)} > \Gamma_{(t-1)} \\ 0 \qquad\qquad : \Gamma_{(t)} \leq \Gamma_{(t-1)} \end{cases} + \begin{cases} P_{(t)} - P_{(t-1)} : P_{(t)} > P_{(t-1)} \\ 0 \qquad\qquad : P_{(t)} \leq P_{(t-1)} \end{cases}$$

MRL(II) models have the potential to encourage more adaptive, multitask learning than MRL(I) models because they do not rely on a reward signal using rules about a fixed set of states and transitions defined prior to learning as the ultimate focus of learning. However, existing models of motivation for MRL(II) models based on novelty and stability do not address the issues of complex, dynamic environments. Novelty-based techniques become problematic in environments that may contain random occurrences since random occurrences often represent phenomena – such as sensor noise – from which little can be learned. The motivational variables predictability, familiarity and stability are general enough to apply to a range of joint control problems. However, the stability variables tie the model specifically to problems in which there is some domain attribute that is required to stabilise over time. In later work, Oudeyer et al. [25] refine their model and introduce Intelligent Adaptive Curiosity as a model of motivation for robots, but they do not use this model in an RL setting.

While a number of researchers have claimed that their HRL and MHRL(I) techniques can be extended for use in MHRL(II) models in the absence of a reward signal [11, 12], in practice there are few theoretic or empirical results regarding such systems. Furthermore, existing performance metrics and baselines become inappropriate in the MHRL(II) setting where the goal is to focus attention for adaptable, multitask learning, rather than to speed up learning.

3.4 Summary

In the most general sense, RL is a computational approach to learning from interaction with an environment using a reward signal to direct learning. A variety of different learning techniques fall within the class of RL algorithms, for addressing episodic or continuous environments, fully or partially observable environments, environments with large state spaces and environments with repeated substructures.

MRL introduces a motivation signal into the RL framework. In existing work, motivation has been characterised in a number of different ways, ranging from rules about the learning domain to computational models of novelty or curiosity. This chapter has classified MRL algorithms into two broad categories: MRL(I) algorithms that incorporate a motivation signal in addition to a reward signal and MRL(II) algorithms that use a motivation signal instead of a reward signal. Within these categories, motivation has been used for a range of different purposes. A number of models use motivation as a means of subtask identification in HRL to speed up learning in environments with repeatable substructures. Other models use motivation as an exploration mechanism either to facilitate later exploitation or to direct action while waiting for reward.

The MRL models introduced in this book use RL to solve tasks identified by computational models of motivation to achieve characters with adaptive, multitask, lifelong learning. In particular, we will focus on MRL(II) models for achieving NPCs capable of adaptive, online learning. A number of components of existing RL approaches are necessary to achieve these goals. Temporal difference learning methods, for example, are most appropriate for lifelong learning as they can learn directly from experience without a model of an environment's dynamics. In addition, non-episodic learning without resets facilitates attention focus in RL by allowing behavioural cycles to emerge within the learned policy.

The next chapter formally introduces the idea of a behavioural cycle and studies ways that the behaviour of NPCs and learning agents can be evaluated and compared.

3.5 References

[1] N.J. Nilsson, Introduction to machine learning, http://ai.stanford.edu/people/nilsson/mlbook.html (Accessed January, 2006), 1996.

[2] R.S. Sutton and A.G. Barto, Reinforcement learning: an introduction, The MIT Press, 2000.

[3] T. Graepel, R. Herbrich and J. Gold, Learning to fight, The International Conference on Computer Games: Artificial Intelligence, Design and Education, 2004.

[4] A.G. Barto and S. Mahadevan, Recent advances in hierarchical reinforcement learning. Discrete Event Dynamic Systems: Theory and Applications 13(4):41–77, 2003.

[5] C. Watkins and P. Dayan, Q-learning. Machine Learning 8(3):279–292, 1992.

[6] D. Precup, R. Sutton and S. Singh, Theoretical results on reinforcement learning with temporally abstract options, The 10th European Conference on Machine Learning, Chemnitz, Germany, Springer Verlag, pp. 382–393, 1998.

[7] S.J. Bradtke and M.O. Duff, Reinforcement learning methods for continuous-time Markov decision problems. In: G. Tesauro, D.S. Touretzky, and T. Leen, (Eds.), Advances in Neural Information Processing Systems: Proceedings of the 1994 Conference, MIT Press, Cambridge, MA, pp. 393–400, 1995.

[8] R. Parr, Hierarchical control and learning for Markov Decision Processes, University of California, Berkeley, 1998.

[9] R. Sutton, D. Precup and S. Singh, Between MDPs and semi-MDPs: A framework for temporal abstraction in reinforcement learning. Artificial Intelligence 112:181–211, 1998.

[10] A. McGovern, Autonomous discovery of temporal abstractions from interaction with an environment, PhD Thesis, Department of Computer Science, University of Massachusetts, 2002.

[11] B. Hengst, Discovering hierarchy in reinforcement learning with HEXQ, The 19th International Conference on Machine Learning, University of New South Wales, Sydney, Australia, pp. 243–250, 2002.

[12] O. Simsek and A.G. Barto, Using relative novelty to identify useful temporal abstractions in reinforcement learning, The 21st International Conference on Machine Learning, Banff, Canada, 2004.

[13] X. Huang and J. Weng, Inherent value systems for autonomous mental development, International Journal of Humanoid Robotics, 4(2):407–433, 2007.

[14] J. Weng and W. Hwang, An incremental learning algorithm with automatically derived discriminating features, Fourth Asian Conference on Computer Vision, Taipei, Taiwan, pp. 426–431, 2000.

[15] J. Schmidhuber, A possibility for implementing curiosity and boredom in model-building neural controllers. In J.A. Meyer, and S.W. Wilson (Eds.), The International Conference on Simulation of Adaptive Behavior: From Animals to Animats, MIT Press/Bradford Books, pp. 222–227, 1991.

[16] J. Schmidhuber, What's interesting, Lugano, Switzerland, 1997.

[17] O. Simsek and A.G. Barto, An intrinsic reward mechanism for efficient exploration, The 23rd International Conference on Machine Learning, University of Pittsburgh, Pennsylvania, USA, 2006.

[18] S. Singh, A.G. Barto and N. Chentanez, Intrinsically motivated reinforcement learning, Advances in Neural Information Processing Systems (NIPS) 17:1281–1288, 2005.

[19] A.G. Barto, S. Singh and N. Chentanez, Intrinsically motivated learning of hierarchical collections of skills, International Conference on Developmental Learning, 2004.

[20] R. Saunders and J.S. Gero, Designing for interest and novelty: motivating design agents, CAAD Futures 2001, Kluwer, Dordrecht, pp. 725–738, 2001.

[21] S. Marsland, U. Nehmzow and J. Shapiro, A real-time novelty detector for a mobile robot, EUREL European Advanced Robotics Systems Masterclass and Conference, 2000.

[22] T. Kohonen, Self-organization and associative memory, Springer, Berlin, 1993.

[23] J.C. Stanley, Computer simulation of a model of habituation. Nature 261:146–148, 1976.

[24] F. Kaplan and P.-Y. Oudeyer, Motivational principles for visual know-how development. In: C.G. Prince, L. Berthouze, H. Kozima, D. Bullock, G. Stojanov and C. Balkenius (Eds.), Proceedings of the 3rd International Workshop on Epigenetic Robotics: Modelling Cognitive Development in Robotic Systems, Lund University Cognitive Studies, pp. 73–80, 2003.

[25] P.-Y. Oudeyer, F. Kaplan and V. Hafner, Intrinsic motivation systems for autonomous mental development. IEEE Transactions on Evolutionary Computation 11(2):265–286, 2007.

Chapter 4
Comparing the Behaviour of Learning Agents

Evaluating the behaviour of non-player characters is a complex problem. The multifaceted goals of non-player characters include:

- believable, realistic or intelligent behaviour;

- support for game flow;

- player engagement and satisfaction.

This list suggests at least three areas for comparing the behaviour of non-player characters: in terms of player satisfaction, in terms of game flow and in terms of the believability or intelligence of the character's behaviour.

This chapter begins by introducing player satisfaction and game flow and the potential role of motivated reinforcement learning in this area. The primary focus of the chapter, however, is on techniques for comparing the action-by-action behaviour of motivated reinforcement learning agents. These techniques aim to provide insight into the characteristics of non-player character behaviour using motivated reinforcement learning. This in turn provides a way to inform the choice of motivated reinforcement learning model for game designers wanting to achieve a particular type of character behaviour.

4.1 Player Satisfaction

Player satisfaction models include cognitive, psychological, affective and empirical models [1, 2]. At the most fundamental level, however, player satisfaction is highly dependent on the objects, non-player characters (NPCs) and layout of the terrain and built environment within a game. These three game elements impact heavily on game flow. Game flow can be considered in two ways: psychological flow and structural flow. Psychological and structural flow are closely related, but structural flow considers flow in terms of the

K.E. Merrick, M.L. Maher, *Motivated Reinforcement Learning*, DOI 10.1007/978-3-540-89187-1_4,
© Springer-Verlag Berlin Heidelberg 2009

layout of game elements, while psychological flow focuses on player ability and the challenge level of the game.

4.1.1 Psychological Flow

The idea of flow was introduced by Csikszentmihalyi to explain happiness in terms of focus in an activity [3]. More recently, the concept of flow has been adapted to computer games [4]. Figure 4.1, introduces the idea of a flow zone for games. Games in the flow zone offer an optimal level of challenge for a player's ability. This avoids player boredom or anxiety and increases enjoyment.

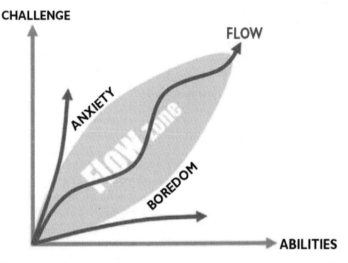

Fig. 4.1 Games in the flow zone offer an optimal level of challenge for a player's ability. This avoids player boredom or anxiety and increases enjoyment [4].

Psychological game flow is calculated as a function of player skills and performance. Modelling NPCs with motivated reinforcement learning (MRL) is relevant to psychological flow because it is a technique with potential application to dynamic difficulty adjustment (DDA). DDA [5] is a form of generative level design that takes into account rules about player skills and performance to adapt the game environment while the game is being played. DDA focuses on maintaining players in their flow zone by adapting the challenge level of the game as players develop their skills. Because MRL agents adapt their behaviour in response to their experiences in their environment, there is also potential for them to adapt to player skill level, although this is not a focus of the models in this book.

4.1.2   Structural Flow

Structural game flow refers to the pacing of a game [6]. For example a game might be short and fast-paced or a long, epic adventure. Structural flow depends on the balance of objects and NPCs and the layout of the terrain and the built environment. For example, games with many resources tend to be faster paced than games that require players to hunt around for required items. Likewise, games with large groups of enemies might be more difficult than games that are sparsely populated with individual monsters. Structural flow is influenced by level layout, including the layout of terrain and buildings and the placement of NPCs and other objects. A number of different categories have been proposed for structural flow models [6, 7], including linear flow, non-linear flow and arenas.

The adaptability of MRL again makes it relevant to structural flow, this time as an approach to procedural content generation (PCG). PCG is the programmatic generation of game content while a game is being played [8]. MRL agents represent an approach to PCG at the character level because the behaviour of MRL agents is generated while the game is in progress.

While game flow and player satisfaction are important means of comparing the high level behaviour of NPCs, this book begins at the action-by-action level. This provides insight into the characteristics NPC behaviour using different MRL models to inform the choice of MRL model for a particular type of NPC.

4.2 Formalising Non-Player Character Behaviour

While different reinforcement learning (RL) models make different assumptions about the learning domain, use different algorithms, and assume different representation techniques, the overall goal of learning new behaviours is common to all models. A comparison of the performance of different models allows a more critical assessment of the strengths and weaknesses of the alternatives. However, in order to compare different RL models, we need to establish a common performance metric.

There are established performance metrics for RL algorithms where the reward is task-specific, but performance metrics for motivated reinforcement learning (MRL) algorithms vary according to the model of motivation and the domain of application. Performance metrics for MRL models tend to occur in two broad categories depending on whether the MRL model is the MRL(I) or MRL(II) type. MRL(I) algorithms, where the motivation value is used in addition to a value returned by the task-specific reward function, are compared to RL algorithms using metrics that make sense for evaluating the performance of RL algorithms without motivation. The metrics appropriate for models that incorporate a task-specific reward signal assume that it is feasible to provide a reward signal for a single, known task and that learning performance can be measured with respect to this task. MRL(II) algorithms, where the motivation value is the driver for learning, do not incorporate a task-specific reward signal so the performance is measured without reference to a specific, known task. Measuring the performance of MRL(II) algorithms has typically been achieved by characterising either the output of the motivation function or the behaviour of the MRL agent.

The remainder of this chapter discusses the existing performance metrics for RL and MRL under these two broad headings: those that measure task-specific learning performance and those which measure other parameters of the model. However, existing metrics in both categories do not adequately capture the adaptive, multitask learning ability of MRL(II) approaches.

4.2.1   Models of Optimality for Reinforcement Learning

A similar set of performance metrics, initially developed for RL, have been applied to RL, HRL and MRL(I) algorithms. These metrics are based on models of optimal behaviour that define how an agent should take the future into account when deciding how to behave. Three models of optimal behaviour used in a majority of RL work are the finite horizon model, the infinite horizon, discounted model and the average reward model [9]. In the finite horizon model an RL agent, at a given moment in time, should optimise its expected reward for the next h time-steps:

$$E\left(\sum_{t=0}^{h} R_{(t)}\right)$$

This model can be used in two ways. In fixed horizon control, the agent initially takes an action that maximises its expected reward for the next h time-steps. It then takes an action that maximises expected reward for the next $h-1$ time-steps and so on. In this case, the agent will have a non-stationary policy. In receding horizon control, the agent always takes an action that maximises reward over the next h time-steps.

The finite horizon model has received some attention. However, it is not always appropriate as it may be difficult to know the length h of an agent's lifetime in advance. The infinite horizon, discounted model avoids this issue by taking into account the long-run reward of the agent. Rewards received in the future are geometrically discounted using a discount factor γ in order to bound the infinite sum:

$$E\left(\sum_{t=0}^{\infty}\gamma^{t}R_{(t)}\right)$$

The average reward model also assumes an infinite horizon, however in this model optimal behavioural policies optimise the long-run average reward of the agent:

$$\lim_{h\to\infty}E\left(\frac{1}{h}\sum_{t=0}^{h}R_{(t)}\right)$$

Such policies are called gain optimal polices and can be thought of as the limiting case of the infinite horizon, discounted model when the value of the discount factor approaches one. A problem with this model is that it does not distinguish between policies that gain high reward in the initial phases and policies that gain reward later.

Many RL algorithms are provably guaranteed to converge asymptotically to one of the three models of optimality described above. In practice, however, algorithms that quickly converge to a near optimal solution may be more useful than algorithms that are guaranteed to converge but do so slowly. As a result, a number of techniques exist to measure the speed of convergence to optimal or near optimal policies. One such technique charts the number of actions performed by an agent against time or the number of learning episodes for a particular task, as shown in Fig. 4.3 below. This gives a visual indication of the speed of convergence of an algorithm to a near optimal policy.

Measuring the speed of convergence to near optimality requires a definition of how near to optimal is sufficient. This is often done on a problem by problem basis. Another related technique for measuring the speed of convergence computes the level of performance of the algorithm after a given time, which similarly requires the definition of the given time. Approaches relating speed of learning to actions performed have an additional weakness in that merely achieving optimality as fast as possible using this measure may incur unnecessarily large reward penalties during the learning period. Less aggressive strategies that take longer to achieve optimality, but gain greater total reward during learning, may be preferable. One alternative technique charts the reward gained by an agent against time or learning episodes, as shown in Fig. 4.2. Another technique, called regret, calculates the expected decrease in reward gained as a result of learning rather than behaving optimally from the start [10]. The techniques used for evaluating the performance of RL algorithms can also be applied to HRL algorithms. RL is often used as a baseline for comparing the speed of convergence of HRL algorithms. For example, in Fig. 4.3 two HRL techniques, HEXQ and MAXQ, are compared to flat RL.

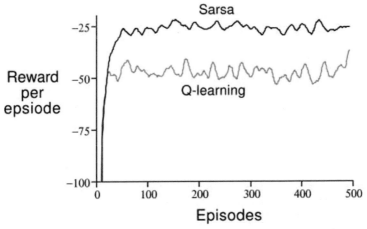

Fig. 4.2 The performance of different reinforcement learning algorithms can be measured as the reward gained in each learning episode. Sutton, Richard S., and Barto, Andrew G., *Reinforcement Learning: An Introduction*, [11] Figure 6.14, © 1998 Massachusetts Institute of Technology, by permission of the MIT Press.

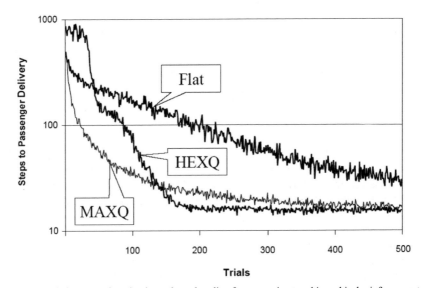

Fig. 4.3 Reinforcement learning is used as a baseline for measuring two hierarchical reinforcement learning algorithms. Performance is measured as the number of steps until the task is complete in each learning episode [12].

The techniques used to evaluate RL have also been applied in MRL(I) settings. Singh et al. [13] use line charts to plot the number of actions in a learned policy against time, as shown in Fig. 4.4(a), while Schmidhuber [14] plots the number of occurrences of rewarded states against time, as shown in Fig. 4.5. Both Singh et al. [13] and Schmidhuber [14] use standard (plain) RL without motivation as a baseline against which to compare their MRL(I) models as shown in Fig. 4.4(b) and Fig. 4.5. These charts allow them to compare the efficiency with which rewarded tasks can be learned.

In Fig. 4.4(a) Singh et al. [13] use a variation of the visualisation in Fig. 4.4(b) to capture the multitask learning capability of MRL(I) agents. Multiple curves are used to visualise learning, one curve for each task. However, this technique does not scale well in complex environments where there are many tasks as the chart becomes cluttered and difficult to interpret. In addition, it is difficult to compare different learning approaches using this technique as each learning agent is characterised by multiple curves.

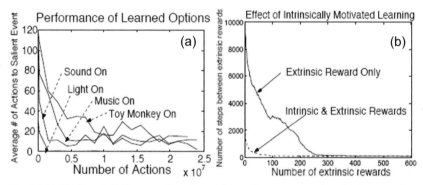

Fig. 4.4 (a) Singh et al. [13] measure learning quality as the average number of actions to salient events. **(b)** Standard reinforcement learning is used as a baseline.

In general, the models of optimality and techniques for measuring the speed of convergence to near optimal solutions are inappropriate for evaluating or comparing the performance of MRL(II) algorithms for two reasons. First, the three models of optimality are based on the assumption that there is a strong relationship between the reward signal and the desired behaviour. That is, they assume that maximising the finite horizon, infinite horizon, discounted or average sum of reward values equates to optimal behaviour with respect to some task or tasks. In RL, HRL and MRL(I) this assumption is feasible as the reward signal is generally hand crafted prior to learning based on knowledge of tasks in the agent's environment. In MRL(II), however, the motivation signal is frequently based on general concepts such as novelty, interest or curiosity and task-oriented behaviour is an emergent property. For MRL(II)

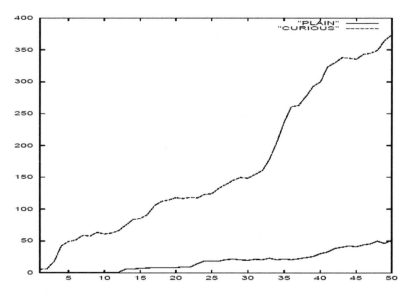

Fig. 4.5 Schmidhuber [14] measures learning quality as the number of occurrences of rewarded 'goal' states. Standard (plain) reinforcement learning is used as a baseline.

algorithms, achieving one of the existing models of optimality no longer implies that task-oriented learning will result.

The second key issue with respect to the application of existing models of optimality to MRL(II) approaches is the assumption in these optimality models that the reward signal is stationary. When the reward signal is stationary, an agent learns the same task or tasks for the duration of its lifetime. Visualisations such as Fig. 4.3 and Fig 4.4(a) that chart the number of actions to reward are appropriate under this assumption as good learning behaviour progressively reduces the number of actions required. However, MRL(II) approaches generally exhibit adaptive, multitask learning in response to a changing reward signal that motivates attention focus on different tasks at different times. In this case, charting the number of actions to reward no longer represents a visualisation of task-oriented learning.

4.2.2   Characteristics of Motivated Reinforcement Learning

As a result of the issues with the models of optimality and performance metrics for RL, a number of different metrics have been developed for MRL(II) algorithms. In contrast to the relatively similar set of techniques used to measure learning performance for RL, HRL and MRL(I) agents, a broad range of different techniques exist for measuring and characterising MRL(II) agents in terms of their motivation functions or learned behaviour. These techniques measure either the output or internal processing stages of the motivation function and thus tend to be specific either to the domain or the motivation function being studied. In the developmental robotics domain, for example, Kaplan and Oudeyer [15] aim to build robotic agents that are able to learn to maintain the stability of head and light source variables in a simple vision application. In order to measure the performance of their algorithm with respect to fulfilling this goal, Kaplan and Oudeyer [15] use line charts to show the evolution of the three motivational variables, predictability, familiarity and stability as shown in Fig. 4.6. They are able to conclude from these charts that their motivation function is successful as predictability, familiarity and stability progressively increase. They then characterise the emergent behaviour of their motivated robotic agents using line charts of physical properties such as head pan position as shown in Fig. 4.7. They conclude that the emergent oscillation between two maxima is desirable as it represents the robot progressively continuing its exploration of its environment.

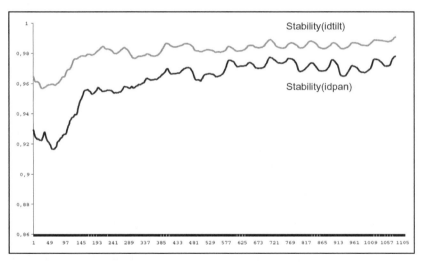

Fig. 4.6 Kaplan and Oudeyer [15] characterise their motivation function in terms of the evolution of its motivational variables: predictability, familiarity, head stability and light stability (shown here).

The charts used by Kaplan and Oudeyer [15] allow them to draw conclusions about the performance of their model for motivating vision related joint manipulation. However, because their metrics are based on explicit internal variables from their motivation process, they are difficult to use as a means of comparing their model to other models, such as the Huang and Weng [16] model, designed for the same type of problem. In addition, Kaplan and Oudeyer [15] are concerned with the behaviour of agents using their model in

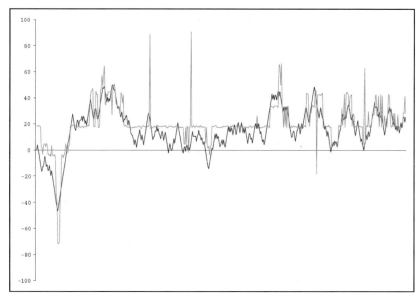

Fig. 4.7 Kaplan and Oudeyer [15] characterise behaviour in terms of domain-specific physical attributes such a head pan position (shown here) and perceived light position.

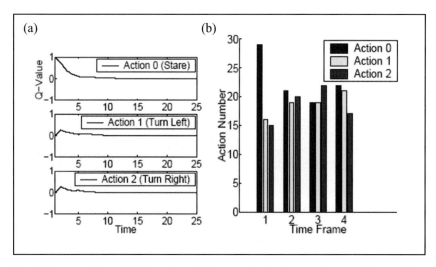

Fig. 4.8 Huang and Weng [16] characterise **(a)** their motivation function in terms of the evolution of Q-values in the learning component and **(b)** behaviour in terms of the frequency with which actions are performed.

a specific playroom domain. Metrics concerned with issues such as head pan position and light position do not necessarily extend to learning in other domains.

In a different approach to characterising the internal performance of a motivation function, Huang and Weng [16] use line charts of the evolution of Q-variables in a table based reinforcement learner to characterise the distribution of the motivation signal as shown in Fig. 4.8(a). They use bar charts to characterise the agent's emergent behaviour in terms of the frequency with which actions are performed as shown in Fig. 4.8(b). This approach allows Huang and Weng [16] to conclude that their robot is displaying desirable emergent behaviour and gives some indication of the efficiency with which that behaviour is learned. However, as $|A| \times |S|$ charts are required to completely represent a learned policy, this technique for measuring performance does not scale well in complex environments with large state or action spaces.

In the design science domain, Saunders and Gero [17] used bar charts to characterise the evolution of novelty within their design agents as shown in Fig. 4.9. The primary goal of the Saunders and Gero [17] model of motivation is to maintain the agent's focus of attention on novel designs. As a result, charting the output of the motivation function and showing its continuing ability to identify novel design solutions is sufficient for measuring the performance of their model. As the work in this book is specifically concerned with measuring the adaptability and multitask learning behaviour of MRL agents, characterising the output of the motivation function is not an applicable metric.

Fig. 4.9 Saunders and Gero [17] characterise their motivation function in terms of the evolution of novelty values.

4.3 Comparing Motivated Reinforcement Learning Agents

In this section we formally introduce the idea of a behavioural cycle to represent and compare the behaviour of NPCs. In existing approaches to NPC design, a behavioural cycle may be the result of animation or the firing of behavioural rules in reflexive agents. MRL extends such approaches to behavioural sequences that can adapt to different tasks at different times in response to changes in an NPC's environment. Thus, to develop learning performance metrics that evaluate adaptive, multitask learning, this section begins by defining mathematically what it means for a behavioural cycle to be learned for a task.

In RL there are two distinct kinds of learning task: maintenance tasks and achievement tasks. Joint manipulation for vision is an example of a maintenance problem. For example, a NPC may need to learn to control its head and neck positions to maintain the stability of visual stimuli. In contrast, the higher level behaviours of NPCs might be achievement tasks. An NPC playing the role of a furniture maker for example, would not merely maintain a state in which it has made furniture, as this would involve making furniture once then doing nothing at all. Rather, a realistic cabinet maker continues to purchase timber and achieve the construction of new items of furniture.

Rhythmic behavioural cycles of states and actions can be illustrated using finite state automata. Figure 4.10(a) shows a behavioural cycle of complexity one for a maintenance task satisfied in the state S_1. Figure 4.10(b) shows a behavioural cycle of complexity n for n achievement tasks satisfied by the transitions between states $S_1 \rightarrow S_2$, $S_2 \rightarrow S_3$ ... $S_n \rightarrow S_1$. The complexity or length of a behavioural cycle refers to the number of actions required to complete a cycle that starts and finishes in a given state.

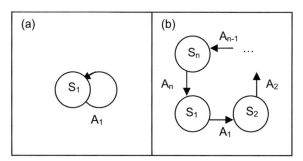

Fig. 4.10 Behavioural cycles of **(a)** complexity one for a maintenance task, **(b)** complexity n for n achievement tasks.

MRL(II) agents may learn a number of different behavioural cycles for different tasks at different periods in their lifetime. Section 4.3.1 introduces a statistical model for identifying such behavioural cycles and the tasks that comprise them. Sects. 4.3.2 and 4.3.3 use this model as a basis for two new metrics that measure adaptive, multitask learning in terms of the variety and complexity of learned tasks.

4.3.1 *Statistical Model for Identifying Learned Tasks*

In order to develop learning performance metrics that evaluate learning in adaptive, multitask learning settings, this section begins by defining mathematically what it means for a task to be learned. A task is denoted by the symbol K. To define when a task is learned, first, the coefficient of variation $c_v(K)$ is computed of the number of actions used to repeat a task K during the last h times the task was performed:

$$c_v(K) = \frac{\sqrt{\dfrac{1}{h-1}\sum_{i=1}^{h}(a_i - \bar{a}_K)^2}}{\bar{a}_K}$$

$\bar{a}_K$ is the mean number of actions required to repeat K during the last h successive repetitions of K. The coefficient of variation represents a normalised measure of the dispersion of the number of actions about the mean $\bar{a}_K$. A task K is learned when the coefficient of variation $c_v(K)$ over the last h solutions of K is less than some error threshold r for the first time.

The use of h solutions of the task K captures the repetitive, cyclic behaviour of MRL. The error term accommodates any noise that might occur in the learning environment. Using this model, charts can be produced that evaluate learning performance as information about $c_v(K)$. The following sections introduce two such metrics: behavioural variety and behavioural complexity.

4.3.2 *Behavioural Variety*

Behavioural variety evaluates the behaviour of an agent by measuring the number of behavioural cycles for different tasks. This measurement is made by analysing the agent's experience trajectory at time t:

$$V_{(t)} = \text{count\_unique}\,(K) \text{ where } c_v(K) < r$$

Instantaneous behavioural variety can be visualised using a bar chart to provide insight into the multitask learning performance of a NPC controlled by a MRL agent. This visualisation characterises multitask learning in terms of the number of tasks learned by a specified time. Because a single agent can be represented by a single series, multiple characters controlled by MRL agents using different motivation components can be compared by plotting a series for each character on the same chart. Figure 4.11 shows an example of such a

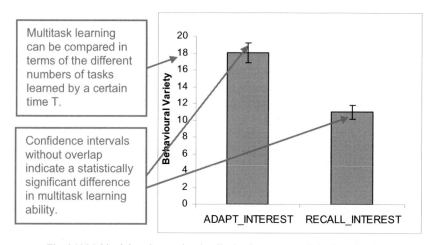

Fig. 4.11 Multitask learning can be visualised as instantaneous behavioural variety.

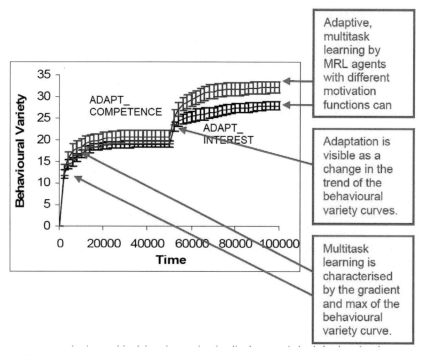

Fig. 4.12 Adaptive, multitask learning can be visualised as cumulative behavioural variety.

comparison for two characters using different MRL models. Error bars show the 95% confidence interval.

Cumulative behavioural variety can be visualised using a line chart with a single series to provide insight into the adaptability or multitask learning performance of a NPC controlled by an MRL agent. This visualisation characterises multitask learning in terms of the gradient and maximum of the curve, which indicates, respectively, the rate at which new tasks are being learned and the number of tasks learned. Adaptability is characterised by changes in the trend of the behavioural variety curve. Because a single agent can be represented by a single series, multiple characters controlled by MRL agents using different motivation or learning components can be compared by plotting a series for each character on the same chart. Figure 4.12 shows an example of such a comparison for two characters using different motivation functions.

4.3.3 Behavioural Complexity

Behavioural complexity evaluates learning performance by measuring the complexity of a learned task in terms of the average length of the behavioural cycle required to repeat the task. More formally, when a task K has been learned according to the definition in Sect. 4.3.1, the complexity X of the task can be measured as the mean numbers of actions $\bar{a}_K$ required to repeat K:

$$X_K = \bar{a}_K$$

Behavioural complexity can be visualised using a bar chart to provide insight into the multitask learning performance of a NPC controlled by a MRL agent. This visualisation characterises multitask learning in terms of the complexity of tasks learned by a specified time. This could include the most complex task learned, the least complex task learned or the average complexity of learned tasks. Because a single agent can be represented by a single series, multiple characters controlled by MRL agents using different motivation or learning components can be compared by plotting a series for each agent on the same chart. Figure 4.13 shows an example of such a comparison for two characters using different motivation functions.

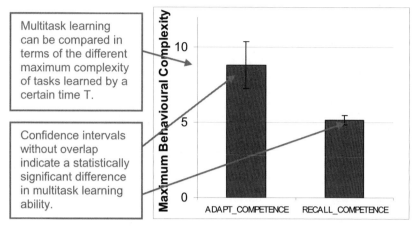

Fig. 4.13 Multitask learning can be visualised in terms of maximum behavioural complexity.

4.4 Summary

The behaviour of NPCs can be analysed in a number of ways including its believability, ability to support game flow and the level of player engagement it achieves. In the long term, MRL has potential as an approach to dynamic difficulty adjustment and procedural content generation to achieve dynamic player satisfaction control. Because MRL agents adapt their behaviour in response to their experiences in their environment, there is also potential for them to adapt to player skill level, thus dynamically modifying game flow and challenge level.

Performance metrics for comparing the action sequences of RL and MRL agents can be classified under two broad headings: those which measure learning performance and those which measure other parameters of the model. Models of optimality and learning performance metrics have tended to be used in RL, HRL and MRL(I) settings while metrics for MRL(II) models have tended to focus on characterising the output of the motivation process or the behaviour of the learning agent.

The focus of this chapter is on techniques for making an action-by-action comparison of the behaviour cycles of MRL agents. These techniques aim to provide insight into the characteristics of NPC behaviour using MRL as a way to inform the choice of MRL model for game designers wanting to achieve a particular type of character behaviour. Part II will present a range of general models from which this choice can be made. Part III will use the behavioural variety and complexity metrics and state automata representations to characterise and compare the behaviour of NPCs using different MRL models.

4.5 References

[1] G.N. Yannakakis and J. Hallam, Towards capturing and enhancing entertainment in computer games, The Fourth Hellenic Conference on Artificial Intelligence, Springer-Verlag, pp. 432–442, 2006.

[2] P. Rani, N. Sarkar and C. Liu, Maintaining optimal challenge in computer games through real-time physiological feedback, HCI International, Las Vegas, USA, 2005.

[3] M. Csikszentmihalyi, Flow: the psychology of optimal experience, Harper Perennial, 1990.

[4] J. Chen, Flow in games (and everything else). Communications of the ACM 50(4):31–34, 2007.

[5] J. Chen, Flow in Games. http://www.jenovachen.com/flowingames/about.htm (Accessed July, 2008).

[6] M. Duggan, The official guide to 3D game studio, Thomson Course Technology, 2007.

[7] E. Byrne, Game level design, Cengage Delmar Learning, 2004.

[8] A. Doull, The death of the level designer: procedural content generation in games. http://roguelikedeveloper.blogspot.com/2008/01/death-of-level-designer-procedural.html (Accessed July, 2008).

[9] L. Kaelbling, M. Littman and A. Moore, Reinforcement learning: a survey. Journal of Artificial Intelligence Research 4:237–285, 1996.

[10] D. Berry and B. Fristedt, Bandit problems: sequential allocation of experiments, Chapman and Hall, London, 1985.

[11] R.S. Sutton and A.G. Barto, Reinforcement learning: an introduction, The MIT Press Cambridge, Massachusetts, London, England, 2000.

[12] B. Hengst, Discovering hierarchy in reinforcement learning with HEXQ, The 19th International Conference on Machine Learning, University of New South Wales, Sydney, Australia, pp. 243–250, 2002.

[13] S. Singh, A.G. Barto and N. Chentanez, Intrinsically motivated reinforcement learning, Advances in Neural Information Processing Systems (NIPS), 17:1281–1288, 2005.

[14] J. Schmidhuber, Exploring the predictable. In A. Ghosh, S. Tsutsui (Eds.), Advances in Evolutionary Computing, pp. 579-612, Springer, 2002.

[15] F. Kaplan and P.-Y. Oudeyer, Motivational principles for visual know-how development. In: C.G. Prince, L. Berthouze, H. Kozima, D. Bullock, G. Stojanov and C. Balkenius (Eds.), Proceedings of the 3rd international workshop on Epigenetic Robotics: Modelling cognitive development in robotic systems, Lund University Cognitive Studies, pp. 73–80, 2003.

[16] X. Huang and J. Weng, Inherent value systems for autonomous mental development, International Journal of Humanoid Robotics, 4(2):407–433, 2007.

[17] R. Saunders and J.S. Gero, Designing for interest and novelty: motivating design agents, CAAD Futures 2001, Kluwer, Dordrecht, pp. 725–738, 2001.

Part II
Developing Curious Characters Using Motivated Reinforcement Learning

Chapter 5
Curiosity, Motivation and Attention Focus

As we develop non-player characters in complex and dynamic game environments, our ability to predefine task specific rules or rewards, or to define environment-specific motivation signals, becomes more unlikely. In such environments, the development of more believable non-player characters will require computational processes that enable the character to focus attention on a relevant portion of the complex environment and to be curious about the changes in the environment. In previous chapters we have shown how reinforcement learning algorithms can automatically generate behaviours. In this chapter we show how concepts of curiosity, motivation, and attention focus can achieve a curious learning agent. We present an agent approach that characterises information outside the agent as the environment, allowing us to conceptualise and model the environment from the perspective of an agent. The agent approach distinguishes between the learner and the environment. After characterising the environment, we then look inside the agent and the motivation process.

An agent that is motivated by changes in the environment has the ability to focus attention on a specific subset of the state representation of the environment as that state changes over time. Motivation as a computational process that drives learning is based on the agent's ability to sense its environment, focus attention on a subset of its sensor data, and calculate a reward for learning as a motivation value. A key concept for curious non-player characters is the development of computational models of curiosity as the motivation function for the agent.

5.1 Agents in Complex, Dynamic Environments

An agent [1] is a computational system that uses sensors to monitor some subset **S** of the world, reasons about the sensed world, and uses a set **A** of actions to trigger effectors that cause transitions to occur in the environment as

K.E. Merrick, M.L. Maher, *Motivated Reinforcement Learning*, DOI 10.1007/978-3-540-89187-1_5,
© Springer-Verlag Berlin Heidelberg 2009

shown in Fig 5.1. Developing agents that can learn in complex, dynamic environments requires a representation of the world or environment states and a flexible labelling structure to accommodate the appearance and disappearance of elements in the environment. This can be achieved with the partially observable Markov decision process (POMDP) formalism and a context free grammar (CFG) [2].

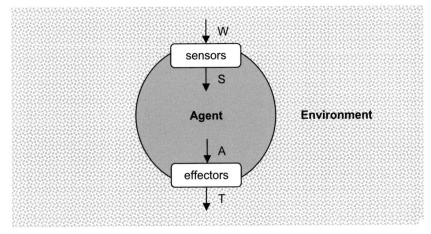

Fig. 5.1 An agent in an environment.

The environment in which an agent is situated is both sensed by the agent and changed by the agent. In the reinforcement learning (RL) formalism, an environment is defined by a set **W** of world states and a set **T** of transitions between world states. Learning in complex, dynamic environments where there is more information in the environment than is relevant to the learner can use the POMDP formalism. In RL, where a reward function guides the selection of the agent's next action, the POMDP consists of:

- a set **W** of world states;
- a set **S** of sensed states;
- a set **A** of actions;
- a reward function $\mathcal{R}$: **W** x **A** x **W** $\rightarrow$ {Reals};
- a transition function $\mathcal{P}$: **W** x **A** x **S** $\rightarrow$ Π (**S**).

$\mathcal{P}$ $(W_{(t+1)}, S_{(t+1)} \mid W_{(t)}, A_{(t)})$ is the probability of making a transition $T_{(t+1)}$ from $W_{(t)}$ to $W_{(t+1)}$ and sensing $S_{(t+1)}$ when the action $A_{(t)}$ is executed. $\mathcal{R}$ $(W_{(t)}, A_{(t)}, W_{(t+1)})$ is the expected reward for the transition $T_{(t+1)}$ and defines a task to be learned.

5.1.1 States

World states $W_{(t)}$ in environments modelled as POMDPs are traditionally represented as fixed-length vectors of attributes: $W_{(t)} = (w_{1(t)}, w_{2(t)}, \ldots w_{|W|(t)})$. Similarly, a sensed state at time t can be represented as a vector of sensations: $S_{(t)} = (s_{1(t)}, s_{2(t)}, \ldots s_{|S|(t)})$. Many virtual environments, however, are made complex by the presence of multiple tasks that may change over time. In these environments only subsets of the state space are relevant to a particular task at a particular time. More formally, we can model such environments as a set of MDPs, **P** as follows:

$$\mathbf{P} = \{P_1, P_2, P_3, \ldots, P_i, \ldots\}$$

The complexity of the environment is defined in terms of the number $|\mathbf{P}|$ of elements in the set **P**. An environment is more complex if the set of MDPs representing it contains more elements. Furthermore, an environment is dynamic if the elements in **P** change over time, either through the addition of new elements or the removal of existing elements.

In dynamic environments, the traditional, fixed-length vector representation for sensations in S becomes inadequate as it does not allow the addition or removal of elements P_i. As an alternative to fixed-length vectors, the sensed states $S_{(t)}$ can be represented as a string from a context-free grammar (CFG) [2] ($\mathbf{V}_S, \mathbf{\Gamma}_S, \mathbf{\Psi}_S, S$) where:

- $\mathbf{V}_S$ is a set of variables or syntactic categories;

- $\mathbf{\Gamma}_S$ is a finite set of terminals such that $\mathbf{V}_S \cap \mathbf{\Gamma}_S = \{\}$;

- $\mathbf{\Psi}_S$ is a set of productions (or rules) of the form $V \rightarrow v$ where V is a variable and v is a string of terminals and variables;

- S is the start symbol.

Thus, the general form of a sensed state is:

```
S                       →     <sensations>
<sensations>            →     <PᵢSensations><sensations>  |  ε
<PᵢSensations>          →     <sⱼ><PᵢSensations>  |  ε
<sⱼ>                    →     <number>  |  <string>
<number>                →     1  |  2  |  3  |  ...
<string>                →     ...
```

This representation is flexible enough to represent environments containing different numbers of elements P_i. This is important in dynamic environments where the elements comprising **P** may change over time. In fixed-length vector representations, two vector states can be compared by comparing the values of vector elements with the same index in each state. In variable-length sensed states, a label L is assigned to each sensation, so that two vector states can be compared by comparing the values of elements that have the same label, where such labels exist. Labels can be constructed using combinations of the grammar terminals in $\mathbf{\Gamma}_S$ and variables in $\mathbf{V}_S$:

$$S = (s_1, s_2, s_3, \ldots s_L, \ldots)$$

5.1.2   Actions

A flexible representation is also required for representing the possible actions that the agent can take in dynamic environments. While agents may only have a fixed set of effectors for the duration of their life, the actions they can then perform may change with the addition or removal of elements P_i from the environment. The action space $\mathbf{A}$ can also be represented using a CFG ($\mathbf{V}_A$, $\mathbf{\Gamma}_A$, $\mathbf{\Psi}_A$, $\mathbf{A}$) where:

- $\mathbf{V}_A$ is a set of variables or syntactic categories;

- $\mathbf{\Gamma}_A$ is a finite set of terminals such that $\mathbf{V}_A \cap \mathbf{\Gamma}_A = \{\}$;

- $\mathbf{\Psi}_A$ is a set of productions of the form $V \rightarrow v$ where V is a variable and v is a string of terminals and variables;

- $\mathbf{A}$ is the start symbol.

Thus, the general form of the action space is:

```
A                  →    <actions>
<actions>          →    <PᵢActions><actions> | ε
<PᵢActions>        →    <Aⱼ><PᵢActions> | ε
<Aⱼ>               →    . . .
```

5.1.3   Reward and Motivation

A reward signal $\mathcal{R}$ is associated with a task in a RL agent and this signal essentially causes the agent to focus attention on a single task to learn a behaviour policy. Traditionally, reward signals have been defined prior to the learning agent interacting with its environment, using a rule-based representation that comprises a set of conditions about subsets of the state space or transition space and numerical values for states or transitions in those subsets. However, a curious learner in complex, dynamic environments may focus on different tasks at different times. Learning a behavioural policy that focuses attention on more than one task requires a reward signal that represents the union of several reward functions $\mathcal{R}_U = \mathcal{R}_a \cup \mathcal{R}_b \cup \mathcal{R}_c \ldots$. Likewise learning a policy that adapts by focusing attention on different tasks at different times, requires a reward signal that represents a progression between different reward signals $\mathcal{R}_P = \mathcal{R}_a \rightarrow \mathcal{R}_b \rightarrow \mathcal{R}_c \ldots$.

Reward signals that represent the union of or progression between reward signals for different tasks using a rule-based approach requires an explicit representation of the conditions for which each reward function and combination of reward functions may be relevant. In complex environments, defining reward functions for each element of **P** is time consuming and requires prior knowledge of large numbers of subsets of the state or transition space, in order to develop the rules that will define each task. In dynamic environments, fixed reward functions may become obsolete if the tasks they define are no longer possible, and new tasks cannot be automatically generated. The role of motivation in RL is to provide an approach to the design of reward signals that approximates the union of, or progression between, reward functions for different tasks – without the need to identify subsets of the state or transition space prior to learning.

Motivation as a process that reasons about an agent's experiences in its environment can produce a motivation signal that is both responsive in dynamic environments and avoids the issues associated with obtaining prior knowledge of state or transition subsets in complex environments. An agent's experiences in a complex, dynamic environment can be modelled as a single, infinite trajectory **Y**. The motivation signal is then an experience-based reward signal. At time t, the process for computing motivation takes the current experience trajectory $\mathbf{Y}_{(t)}$ as input and outputs a motivation value $R_{m(t)}$ as shown below. That is, motivation is a kind of reward signal that is computed as a function of an agent's experiences:

$$R_{m(t)} = \mathcal{R}(\mathbf{Y}_{(t)})$$

5.2 Motivation and Attention Focus

Mathematical models of motivation and attention focus are important for achieving adaptable behavioural cycles and merging motivation with RL. Since the reward signal in RL defines the task to be learned, structures are required to represent and select potential learning tasks as a basis for computing motivation. In RL there are two distinct kinds of learning task: maintenance tasks and achievement tasks. Joint manipulation for vision is an example of a maintenance problem. For example, a NPC may learn to control its head and neck positions to maintain the stability of visual stimuli. In contrast, the higher level tasks required of NPCs are often achievement tasks.

For example, a NPC playing the role of a furniture maker would not merely maintain a state in which it has made furniture, as this would involve making furniture once then doing nothing at all. Rather, a realistic cabinet maker continues to purchase timber and achieve the construction of new items of furniture.

The following sections introduce observations and events for representing potentially motivating maintenance and achievement tasks respectively. We then show how models of unsupervised learning provide an adaptive representation of the subset of tasks currently selected for attention focus. We use two kinds of motivation for learning: interest and competence. Existing mathematical models of the psychological motivation theories describing novelty and interest are combined to compute a motivation value for "interest". In addition, two new formulae are developed for modelling competence as a motivation signal. Finally, arbitration functions are introduced that compute a single reward signal to focus learning and action according to the current tasks and multiple motivation signals of an agent.

5.2.1   Observations

Observations differ from sensed states in that they represent, and thus focus attention on, only potential maintenance tasks. The difference between a world state, sensed state and an observation is illustrated in Fig. 5.2.

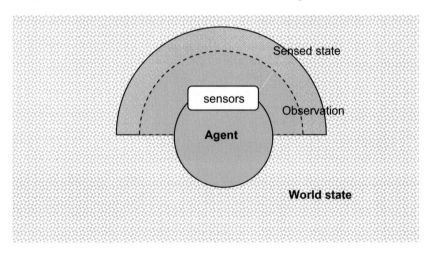

Fig. 5.2. Difference between a world state, a sensed state and an observation.

An observation is essentially a combination of sensations from the sensed state, where a combination is an unordered selection of sensations made without repetition. There are $2^{|S_{(t)}|} - 1$ possible combinations of sensations. For an agent to function efficiently in complex environments where $|S_{(t)}|$ is large it may be necessary to select only a subset of these combinations as observations. This subset is defined by an observation function mapping the sensed state $S_{(t)}$ to a set of observations $\mathbf{O}_{S(t)}$.

Observation Functions

Observation functions define the combinations of sensations from the sensed state that will motivate further reasoning. Observations containing fewer sensations affect an agent's attention focus by making it possible for the agent to restrict its attention to a subset of the state space. Observations containing fewer sensations have greater spatial selectivity as they describe only a small proportion of the state space. Conversely, observations containing more sensations have lower spatial selectivity because they describe a greater proportion of the state space. Observation functions that represent two extremes of attention focus are shown in Table 5.1. The first function displays high spatial selectivity, with each observation containing only one sensation. In contrast, the second function displays lower spatial selectivity as each observation focuses attention on every element of the sensed state. Like the sensed states from which they are computed, observations may be of varying length.

Table 5.1 Observation functions that achieve different levels of attention focus at time t.

	Observation Function 1	Observation Function 2
Observations Recognised $\mathbf{O}_{S(t)}$	$O_{1(t)} = (o_{1(t)}, 0, 0, 0, \ldots)$ $O_{2(t)} = (0, o_{2(t)}, 0, 0, \ldots)$ $\ldots$ $O_{L(t)} = (0, \ldots, o_{L(t)}, 0, \ldots)$ $\ldots$	$O_{1(t)} = (o_{1(t)}, o_{2(t)}, \ldots, o_{L(t)}, \ldots)$
Rule	$o_{i(t)} = \begin{cases} s_{i(t)} & \text{if } i = L \\ 0 & \text{otherwise} \end{cases}$	$o_{L(t)} = s_{L(t)}$
Number of Observations	$|O_{(t)}|$	1
Attention Focus	High: each observation focuses on one sensation.	Low: each observation focuses on all sensations.

5.2.2 Events

In order to represent potentially motivating achievement tasks on which attention may be focused, we introduce events to model the transitions between sensed states. Events differ from actions in that a single action may cause a number of different transitions, depending on the situation in which it is performed while an event describes a specific transition. Events enable attention focus on the actual transition that results from an action by modelling the difference between successive sensed states. Events are computed using difference functions and event functions that control the level of attention focus on the transition.

Events are represented in terms of the difference between two sensed states. The difference between two sensed states, $S_{(t')} = (s_{1(t')}, s_{2(t')}, \ldots s_{L(t')} \ldots)$ and $S_{(t)} = (s_{1(t)}, s_{2(t)}, \ldots s_{L(t)} \ldots)$ where $t' < t$ as a vector of difference variables is calculated using a difference function Δ as follows:

$$S_{(t)} - S_{(t')} = (\Delta(s_{1(t)}, s_{1(t')}), \Delta(s_{2(t)}, s_{2(t')}), \ldots, \Delta(s_{L(t)}, s_{L(t')}), \ldots)$$

An event is a combination of difference variables. A combination is an unordered selection of difference variables made without repetition. There are $2^{|S_{(t)} - S_{(t')}|} - 1$ possible combinations of difference variables. For an agent to function efficiently in environments where $|S_{(t)} - S_{(t')}|$ is large it may be necessary to select only a subset of these combinations as events. This subset is defined by an event function mapping the difference $S_{(t)} - S_{(t')}$ to a set of events $\mathbf{E}_{S_{(t)}}$.

Difference Functions

A difference function Δ assigns a value to the difference between two sensations $s_{L(t)}$ and $s_{L(t')}$ in the sensed states $S_{(t)}$ and $S_{(t')}$. A number of difference functions that achieve different degrees of attention focus are presented in Table 5.2. Difference Function 1 offers the most information about the change between successive sensations as it calculates the magnitude and direction of the change. In contrast, Difference Function 2 focuses only on the direction of the change. Difference Function 3 is the most focused difference function, showing only whether or not a change has occurred. Such a difference function might be useful in situations where a numerical difference is not meaningful, for example, when comparing the difference between two sensations with string values rather than numeric values. A difference function similar to Difference Function 3 was used by Singh et al. [3], who define a salient event as any change in light or sound intensity, regardless of the magnitude of that change.

Table 5.2 Difference functions that achieve different levels of attention focus at time t.

	Difference Function 1	Difference Function 2	Difference Function 3
$\Delta(s_{L(t)}, s_{L(t')})$	$\begin{cases} s_{L(t)} \text{ if } \neg\exists\ s_{L(t')} \\ -s_{L(t')} \text{ if } \neg\exists\ s_{L(t)} \\ s_{L(t)} - s_{L(t')} \text{ if } s_{L(t)} - s_{L(t')} \neq 0 \\ \text{null otherwise} \end{cases}$	$\begin{cases} 1 \text{ if } s_{L(t)} > s_{L(t')} \\ -1 \text{ if } s_{L(t)} < s_{L(t')} \\ \text{null otherwise} \end{cases}$	$\begin{cases} 1 \text{ if } s_{L(t)} = s_{L(t')} \\ \text{null otherwise} \end{cases}$
Output Range	$(-\infty, \infty)$	$\{-1, 1\}$	$\{1\}$
Attention Focus	Low: all information about the size of and direction of change in a sensation is available.	Moderate: attention focused on whether a sensation has increased or decreased.	High: attention focused only on whether a sensation has changed or not.

Table 5.3 Event functions that achieve different levels of attention focus at time t.

	Event Function 1	Event Function 2
Events Recognised $E_{S(t)}$	$E_{1(t)} = (\Delta(s_{1(t)}, s_{1(t')}), 0, 0, 0, \ldots)$ $E_{2(t)} = (0, \Delta(s_{2(t)}, s_{2(t')}), 0, 0, \ldots)$ $\ldots$ $E_{L(t)} = (0, \ldots, \Delta(s_{L(t)}, s_{L(t')}), 0, \ldots)$ $\ldots$	$E_{1(t)} = (e_{1(t)}, e_{2(t)}, \ldots e_{L(t)} \ldots)$
Rule	$e_{e(t)} = \begin{cases} \Delta(s_{e(t)}, s_{e(t')}) \text{ if } e = L \\ 0 \text{ otherwise} \end{cases}$	$e_{L(t)} = \Delta(s_{L(t)}, s_{L(t')})$
Number of Events	$|S_{(t)} - S_{(t')}|$	1
Attention Focus	High: each event focuses on one difference.	Low: each event focuses on all differences

Event Functions

Event functions define which combinations of difference variables an agent recognises as events. Events containing fewer difference variables affect an agent's attention focus by making it possible for the agent to restrict its attention to a subset of the transition space. Events containing fewer difference variables have greater spatial selectivity as they describe changes in only a small proportion of the state space. Conversely, events containing more difference variables have lower spatial selectivity because they describe changes in a greater number of sensations and thus a greater proportion of the state space. Event functions that represent two extremes of attention focus are shown in Table 5.3. The first function displays high spatial selectivity, with each event containing only one non-zero difference variable. In contrast, the second function displays lower spatial selectivity as each event focuses attention on every difference variable. Like the sensed states from which they are computed, events may be of varying length or even empty, depending on the number of sensations to change. Events may also be normalised for input to a task selection process.

5.2.3   Tasks and Task Selection

The introduction of observations and events to represent potential maintenance and achievement tasks implies a new representation of agent experiences in which the state, action and motivation trajectories are augmented with observation set and event set trajectories as follows:

$$\mathbf{Y}_{(t)} = S_{(1)}, \mathbf{O}_{S(1)}, \mathbf{E}_{S(1)}, A_{(1)}, S_{(2)}, \mathbf{O}_{S(2)}, \mathbf{E}_{S(2)}, A_{(2)}, \ldots, S_{(t)}, \mathbf{O}_{S(t)}, \mathbf{E}_{S(t)}, A_{(t)}$$

The observation and event set trajectories comprise all potential learning tasks (observations and events) on which the agent may focus attention. Individual tasks are solved each time the observation or event representing them occurs.

During lifelong learning in complex environments, agents encounter large numbers of tasks. Furthermore, in dynamic environments tasks identified in the past may no longer be relevant at the current time-step. In order to facilitate MRL that achieves adaptive learning in complex, dynamic environments, it is an advantage to focus attention on a subset of tasks as a basis for computing the motivation signal. Saunders [4] suggests two reasonable assumptions for modelling subsets of an experience trajectory: first that recent experiences are likely to be the most relevant at the current time, and secondly that similar experiences from any time in the past are likely to be relevant for determining what actions to take in the present. These assumptions are adopted as guidelines for the definition of task selection functions that support the emergence of adaptive behavioural cycles for multitask learning.

Task selection functions map the set $\mathbf{O}_{S(t)} \cup \mathbf{E}_{S(t)}$ ($\forall\, t$) of all potential learning tasks to a set $\mathbf{K}$ of tasks to learn. The motivation and arbitration functions then combine to produce a motivation signal that focuses learning on those tasks. A simplistic approach to task selection might be to use a history window over the observation and event set trajectories to select tasks to learn, however using this approach, observations or events outside the history window do not influence the current task selection. Alternatively, task selection functions that identify recently experienced tasks while taking into account similar past experiences are well modelled using certain incremental unsupervised learning (UL) or data-stream mining algorithms.

Self-organising maps (SOMs) are one example of an unsupervised learning algorithm that can be modified for use as a task selection function. SOMs comprise a number of neurons that represent clusters of input data. When used as a task selection function, SOM neurons represent the current set **K** of tasks to learn and observations and/or events are input for the SOM. The SOM update function progressively modifies each neuron K to model tasks that are relevant to the most recent observations or events, but also influenced by past observations or events. A SOM can be adapted to process variable length inputs such as observations and events by initialising each neuron K as a zero-length vector $K = ( )$. Each time a stimulus observation $O_{(t)}$ (or event $E_{(t)}$) is presented to the SOM, each neuron is updated by adding randomly initialised variables k_L with any labels L that occur in $O_{(t)}$ (or $E_{(t)}$) but not in K. The most similar task model is then further updated by selecting the neuron $K_{(t)}$ with the minimum distance d to the input stimulus where d is calculated using the SOM distance function, modified to accept variable-length events by incorporating a difference function as follows:

$$d = \sqrt{\sum_L \Delta(k_{L(t)}, o_{L(t)})^2}$$

All neurons in the neighbourhood of the chosen task model are then moved closer to the input stimulus by adjusting each of their weights k_L using the SOM update equation, again modified to incorporate the difference function:

$$k_{L(t+1)} = k_{L(t)} + \eta \, \Delta(o_{L(t)}, k_{L(t)})$$

where $0 \leq \eta \leq 1$ is the learning rate of the SOM. The SOM neighbourhood function imbues the learned network with the useful property that even non-winning neurons may contain some information about tasks as a result of being updated by the neighbourhood function. This allows the network to better model tasks with which it has never previously been presented. The SOM neighbourhood function has, however, an undesirable network dragging effect that occurs when progressively presented inputs have only small differences. This has the effect of reducing the number of task models that emerge in slowly changing environments. In these environments, other unsupervised learning techniques, such as K-means clustering, offer a useful alternative as a task selection function.

K-means clustering uses a set of centroids to represent clusters of input data. When K-means clustering is used as a task selection function, these centroids represent the current set **K** of tasks to learn and observations and/or events represent input. The K-means update function progressively modifies each centroid K to model tasks that are relevant to the most recent observations or events, while influenced by past observations or events. K-means clustering can be adapted to reason about variable length inputs such as observations and events by initialising each centroid K as a zero length vector. Each time a stimulus observation $O_{(t)}$ (or event $E_{(t)}$) is available, each centroid is lengthened by adding randomly initialised variables k_L with any labels L that occur in $O_{(t)}$ (or $E_{(t)}$) but not in K. The most similar task model is updated by selecting the centroid $K_{(t)}$ with the minimum distance d to the input stimulus where d is calculated using the K-means distance function, modified to accept variable-length events by incorporating a difference function as follows:

$$d = \sqrt{\sum_L \Delta(k_{L(t)}, o_{L(t)})^2}$$

The centroid $K_{(t)}$ is then moved closer to the input stimulus by adjusting each of its weights k_L using the update equation, again modified to incorporate the difference function:

$$k_{L(t+1)} = k_{L(t)} + \eta\, \Delta(o_{L(t)}, k_{L(t)})$$

where $0 \leq \eta \leq 1$ is again the learning rate. Once learning tasks have been selected, it remains to compute a motivation signal to focus learning and action on these tasks.

5.2.4   Experience-Based Reward as Cognitive Motivation

A wide variety of techniques have previously been referred to as motivation functions for artificial systems. These range from domain-based rules to computational models of psychological motivation theories. Here we focus specifically on the psychologically inspired models of motivation as a starting point for developing artificial systems that display the emergent behavioural cycles and adaptive, multitask learning that are characteristic of attention focus in natural systems. As the input for these motivation functions represents potential learning tasks identified based on experiences, this work is further focused on the development of cognitively inspired models of motivation. Cognitive theories of motivation are abstracted from the biological structures of an organism and thus offer a starting point for the development of computational models of motivation based on abstract concepts such as tasks. First, a number of existing cognitively inspired computational models of motivation are described that can be adapted for use as experience-based reward functions for MRL. Two further models are described that introduce introspection specifically tailored to MRL. The use of a common framework based on observations and events provides a basis for extending existing MRL research by comparing and evaluating the performance of different motivation functions.

Marsland's real-time novelty detector [5] is an example of a cognitively inspired computational model of motivation that can be modified for use in a MRL setting. A real-time novelty detector models novelty using a SOM for task selection with an additional layer of habituating neurons to compute a habituated novelty value. The activities of the winning neuron and its neighbours in the SOM are propagated up the synapse to the habituating layer as a synaptic value $\varsigma_{(t)} = 1$. Neurons that do not belong to the winning neighbourhood give an input of $\varsigma_{(t)} = 0$ to the synapse.[2] The synaptic efficacy or novelty $N_{(t)}$ of each task model is then calculated using Stanley's model of habituation [6] with the appropriate synaptic value:

$$\tau \frac{dN_{(t)}}{dt} = \alpha \left[N_{(0)} - N_{(t)} \right] - \varsigma_{(t)}$$

$N_{(0)} = 1$ is the initial novelty value of each task model, τ is a constant governing the rate of habituation and α is a constant governing the rate of recovery. $N_{(t)}$ is calculated stepwise at time t by using the value $N_{(t-1)}$ stored in the habituating neuron to calculate the derivative from the equation above and then approximating $N_{(t)}$ as follows:

$$N_{(t)} = N_{(t-1)} + \frac{dN_{(t-1)}}{dt}$$

Habituated novelty values decrease with repeated presentation of similar stimuli. When such stimuli are removed or different stimuli are presented, novelty values recover as shown in Fig. 5.3. This has the potential to promote the emergence of rhythmic behavioural cycles in MRL.

---

[2] Marsland et al. [5] suggest using a synaptic value $\varsigma_{(t)} = d$ for the winning neighbourhood. However, in environments where the probability of each state transition does not change, the SOM is able to cluster input vectors with progressively increasing accuracy so $\lim_{t \to \infty} d = 0$. This has the effect of inhibiting the habituation process as time passes and damping the change in novelty.

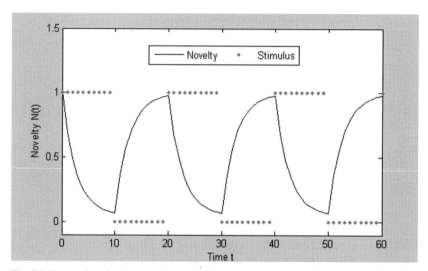

Fig. 5.3 The novelty of a stimulus decreases with repeated exposure to the stimulus (habituation). Novelty increases when the stimulus is removed (recovery).

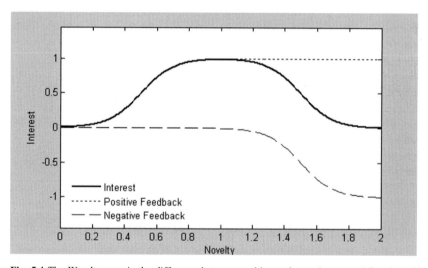

Fig. 5.4 The Wundt curve is the difference between positive and negative reward functions. It peaks at a moderate degree of novelty.

A real-time novelty detector can be adapted for use in the MRL framework by using the modified SOM described in Sect. 5.2.3 in place of the standard SOM, and observations and/or events as input. However, while novelty is a useful motivator in some environments, in complex, dynamic environments there is often a possibility of random observations or events as a result of either the environment dynamics or sensor noise. Novelty can be a poor motivator for RL in such environments as random occurrences tend to be highly novel but offer little opportunity to learn. The computational model of interest developed by Saunders [4] offers an alternative to novelty that avoids this problem.

Saunders [4] modelled interest by first using a real-time novelty detector to compute the novelty of a stimulus, then applying the Wundt curve as follows:

$$\mathcal{R}(N_{(t)}) = \mathcal{F}^+(N_{(t)}) - \mathcal{F}^-(N_{(t)}) = \frac{F^+_{max}}{1 + e^{-\rho^+ (2N_{(t)} - F^+_{min})}} - \frac{F^-_{max}}{1 + e^{-\rho^- (2N_{(t)} - F^-_{min})}}$$

The Wundt curve provides positive reward $\mathcal{F}^+$ for the discovery of novel stimuli and negative reward $\mathcal{F}^-$ for highly novel stimuli. It peaks at a maximum value for a moderate degree of stimulation – as shown in Fig. 5.4 – meaning that the most interesting events are those that are similar-yet-different to previously encountered experiences. F^+_{max} is the maximum positive reward, F^-_{max} is the maximum negative reward, ρ^+ and ρ^- are the slopes of the positive and negative reward sigmoid functions, F^+_{min} is the minimum novelty to receive positive reward and F^-_{min} is the minimum novelty to receive negative reward.

Like a real-time novelty detector, the Saunders [4] model of interest can be modified for use in the MRL framework by using the modified SOM in place of the standard SOM and observations and/or events as input. This model offers a starting point for introducing extrospective motivation into a RL setting in complex, dynamic environments. Extrospective models of motivation for which experiences in the environment are used as input are important for modelling motivation that is responsive to changes in the environment. However, extrospective motivation alone only indirectly reasons about the learning process by reasoning about the states and actions that define the learned behavioural cycles. When motivation is not strongly linked with the learning process, attention focus may shift too rapidly for stable behavioural cycles to emerge. If behavioural cycles stabilise too slowly, behaviour will appear unresponsive to change.

Introspective motivation functions compute motivation values using experiences other than or in addition to experiences from the environment. In

MRL this data may include trajectories of learned policies and their properties, past motivation values or past actions. The experience trajectory becomes:

$$\mathbf{Y}_{(t)} = S_{(1)}, \mathbf{O}_{S(1)}, \mathbf{E}_{S(1)}, \pi_{(1)}, \mathbf{B}_{(1)}, A_{(1)}, R_{m(1)}, S_{(2)}, \mathbf{O}_{S(2)}, \mathbf{E}_{S(2)}, \pi_{(2)}, \mathbf{B}_{(2)}, A_{(2)}, R_{m(2)},$$
$$\dots, S_{(t)}, \mathbf{O}_{S(t)}, \mathbf{E}_{S(t)}, \pi_{(t)}, \mathbf{B}_{(t)}, A_{(t)}, R_{m(t)}$$

Two introspective motivation functions are proposed for MRL based on the concept of competence. The first model is inspired by White's [7] theory of effectance motivation. White describes effectance or competence motivation as the desire to deal effectively with one's environment. Competence motivation is defined here for tasks in MRL in terms of the maximum error in a learned behavioural cycle that includes those tasks. Competence motivation is modelled using the modified SOM for task selection with an additional layer of error neurons to compute a competence value. In TD learning, the error between the portion of the former policy being updated and the new policy is:

$$\Delta Q_{(t)} = |Q_{(t)}(S_{(t)}, A_{(t)}) - Q_{(t-1)}(S_{(t)}, A_{(t)})|$$

Each time a stimulus observation or event occurs, the activities of the winning neuron and its neighbours in the SOM are propagated up the synapse to the error layer as a synaptic value $\varsigma_{(t)} = \Delta Q_{(t)}$. Each neuron K_{err} in the error layer is updated to contain the maximum error value propagated up the synapse during the current behavioural cycle:

$$K_{err} = \begin{cases} \varsigma_{(t)} \text{if } \varsigma_{(t)} > K_{err(t-1)} \\ K_{err(t-1)} \text{ otherwise} \end{cases}$$

Competency $C_{(t)}$ for the current observation or event is inversely proportional to the value stored in the error neuron $K_{err(t)}$ for the winning task model $K_{(t)}$ for that stimulus:

$$C_{(t)} = \frac{1}{K_{err(t)}}$$

Each $K_{err(t)}$ is then reset to zero representing the start of a new behavioural cycle for the current task. Using this model, competence is highest when error is lowest and lowest when error is highest as shown in Fig. 5.5. While this model of motivation, like novelty, is useful in certain environments, in complex, dynamic environments, where there is a possibility of random observations or events, competence alone can be a poor motivator of RL. Agents tend to have low competence at random occurrences but there is also little opportunity to learn from such occurrences.

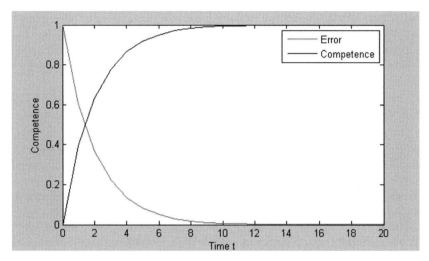

Fig. 5.5 Learning error and competence have an inverse relationship.

The second introspective motivation function modifies the model of competence motivation using the theory of intrinsic motivation proposed by Deci and Ryan [8] as inspiration. Deci and Ryan [8] proposed that individuals are involved in an ongoing, cyclical process of seeking out or creating optimally challenging situations and then attempting to conquer those challenges. A feeling of competence emerges from situations in which an individual is optimally challenged. The situations that are most intrinsically motivating are those that contain information relevant to structures already stored and mastered but that are discrepant enough to call forth adaptive modifications.

Optimal challenges are modelled using the Wundt curve applied to the model of competence motivation. The Wundt curve provides positive reward $\mathcal{F}^+$ for the discovery of tasks at which the agent is not competent and negative reward $\mathcal{F}^-$ for tasks at which the agent is highly competent. It peaks at a maximum value for a moderate degree of competence, meaning that optimally challenging tasks are those at which the agent already has moderate competence. F_{max}^+ is again the maximum positive reward, F_{max}^- the maximum negative reward, ρ^+ and ρ^- the slopes of the positive and negative reward sigmoid functions, F_{min}^+ the minimum competence to receive positive reward and F_{min}^- is the minimum competence to receive negative reward.

$$\mathcal{R}(C_{(t)}) = \mathcal{F}^+(C_{(t)}) - \mathcal{F}^-(C_{(t)}) = \frac{F_{max}^+}{1 + e^{-\rho^+(2C_{(t)} - F_{min}^+)}} - \frac{F_{max}^-}{1 + e^{-\rho^-(2C_{(t)} - F_{min}^-)}}$$

Motivation using this model peaks for a moderate degree of competence, implying that some other motivation is required to initiate learning. When several motivations compete or co-operate to focus attention, arbitration functions are required to produce a scalar motivation signal.

5.2.5   *Arbitration Functions*

When an agent is reasoning about a single task using a single motivation function, the motivation value computed by that motivation function, using the task as input, may be used directly as the reward signal forwarded to the learning process. However, when more than one motivation function is used or more than one task is selected at each time-step, the motivation signal $R_{m(t)}$ output by the motivation process is computed by a function that arbitrates between the motivation values produced for different tasks or by different motivation functions. Two examples of possible arbitration functions for combining the effects of multiple models of motivation are shown in Table 5.4. The first arbitration function provides a means by which conflicting motivations can compete to influence learning. Motivation is modelled as the maximum value from all experience-based reward functions. This means that a single motivating factor will influence learning at any time-step. The second arbitration function provides a means by which motivations can cooperate to influence learning. It models motivation as a weighted sum of values for a given event. Using this function, several motivating factors may influence learning at any time-step.

Three examples of possible arbitration functions for multiple tasks are shown in Table 5.5. The first arbitration function provides a means by which a decision can be made between conflicting tasks. It models motivation as the maximum value of any task. This means that attention will be focused on a single motivating task that will influence learning. The second and third arbitration functions model motivation for tasks that can be performed together. Motivation is modelled as the average value for all tasks and as a weighted sum. Using these functions, attention may be focused on several tasks that will influence learning at each time-step.

Table 5.4 Arbitration functions for producing a motivation signal from motivation values, when motivation values are computed by multiple computational models of motivation.

Arbitration Function 1	Arbitration Function 2
$R_{m(t)} = \max\limits_{i} \, \mathcal{R}_i(K_{(t)})$	$R_{m(t)} = \sum\limits_{i} w_i \mathcal{R}_i(K_{(t)})$
Motivations compete to influences learning.	Motivations co-operate to influence learning.

Table 5.5. Arbitration functions for producing a motivation signal from motivation values, when motivation values are computed for multiple motivating tasks.

Arbitration Function 1	Arbitration Function 2	Arbitration Function 3
$R_{m(t)} = \max\limits_{K \in \mathbf{K}_{S(t)}} \mathcal{R}(K)$	$R_{m(t)} = \operatorname*{avg}\limits_{K \in \mathbf{K}_{S(t)}} \mathcal{R}(K)$	$R_{m(t)} = \sum\limits_{K_i \in \mathbf{K}_{S(t)}} w_i \mathcal{R}(K)$
Tasks compete to motivate learning.	Tasks cooperate equally to motivate learning.	Tasks cooperate to motivate learning.

5.2.6 A General Experience-Based Motivation Function

We now have all of the key ingredients for generating a motivation signal to reward learning for an agent in a complex, dynamic environment. Here we put it all together to develop a computational process that generates a motivation signal based on an agent's experiences in a complex, dynamic environment. This motivation signal is the driver for learning in a motivated reinforcement learning agent.

Recall that the agent's experience is modelled as a single, infinite trajectory **Y**. This trajectory may comprise extrospective experiences of the environment or introspective experiences from the learning process. Possible constituent trajectories of **Y** are summarised in Table 5.6.

The algorithm for modelling motivation for experience-based attention focus is shown in Fig. 5.6 and represented diagrammatically in Fig. 5.7. Observations computed by an observation function (line 1) represent potential maintenance tasks. Events computed using difference and event functions (lines 2–3) represent potential achievement tasks. Task selection (line 4) identifies a subset of learning tasks. One or more experience-based motivation signals are then used to compute values that focus attention on certain tasks (lines 5–7). These values are combined using an arbitration function (line 8) that computes a single motivation signal. This value and the sensed state are then passed to the RL process.

Table 5.6 Potential experience trajectories as input for motivation functions in motivated reinforcement learning.

Experience Trajectory	Description	Attention Focus
$S_{(t)}, S_{(t+1)}, S_{(t+2)}, \dots$	Sensed state trajectory	Influenced by
$\mathbf{O}_{S(t)}, \mathbf{O}_{S(t+1)}, \mathbf{O}_{S(t+2)}, \dots$	Observation set trajectory	experiences from the
$\mathbf{E}_{S(t)}, \mathbf{E}_{S(t+1)}, \mathbf{E}_{S(t+2)}, \dots$	Event set trajectory	environment.
$R_{m(t)}, R_{m(t+1)}, R_{m(t+2)}, \dots$	Motivation trajectory	
$A_{(t)}, A_{(t+1)}, A_{(t+2)}, \dots$	Action trajectory	Influenced by
$\pi_{(t)}, \pi_{(t+1)}, \pi_{(t+2)}, \dots$	Policy trajectory	introspective
$\mathbf{B}_{(t)}, \mathbf{B}_{(t+1)}, \mathbf{B}_{(t+2)}, \dots$	Option set trajectory	experiences.

```
1. Observe Oₛ₍ₜ₎ from S₍ₜ₎ using the observation function
2. Subtract S₍ₜ₎ - S₍ₜ'₎ using the difference function
3. Compose Eₛ₍ₜ₎ using the event function
4. Distinguish Kₛ₍ₜ₎ using the task selection function
5. Repeat (for each Kᵢ ∈ K₍ₜ₎):
6.        Repeat (for each Rⱼ ∈ R):
7.                Compute ℜⱼ(Kᵢ) using experience-based reward fn Rⱼ
8. Arbitrate over ℜⱼ(Kᵢ) ∀ i,j to produce Rₘ₍ₜ₎
```

Fig. 5.6 Algorithmic description of motivation for attention focus in reinforcement learning.

The model of experience-based motivation shown here differs from existing models in that it provides a general approach to the representation of tasks, task selection, experience-based reward and arbitration. This provides a basis for experimenting with different combinations of psychological motivation theories. This general model does not, however, answer all questions with respect to the design of computational models for specific motivation theories. In this model, the representation of tasks must be fixed prior to the agent interacting with its environment to support reasoning about the types of learning task present in the environment. While general representations that capture many types of learning task can be chosen, this increases the time and memory requirements for reasoning. The unsupervised learning algorithms used in the task-selection phase also require certain parameters to be fixed prior to an agent interacting with its environment. An HSOM, for example, has a fixed number of neurons while K-means clustering requires a value of $|K|$, the number of neurons, to be defined prior to learning. Some alternative techniques such as ART maps [9] increase the number of neurons automatically, but parameters such as the network learning rate must still be fixed prior to learning.

The adaptable CFG representation of the environment provides a model for extending MRL to dynamic environments. Existing unsupervised learning algorithms can be adapted as task selection processes that take variable-length observations or events in CFG representation as input. The key change made to existing SOM and K-means algorithms is to allow neurons or centroids to expand automatically when new elements of observations or events are sensed. The issue of allowing neurons or centroids to contract or forget elements that have not been sensed for some period is not addressed. This issue becomes relevant in environments with large state spaces that change over time such that some subsets of the state space are no longer important for reasoning.

The model of motivation presented above is designed as a process that is largely independent of the learning process. Interaction between the two processes is limited to shared memory and the motivation signal output by the motivation process that becomes input for the learning process. This ensures that the motivation process is flexible enough to be incorporated in a number of different RL settings. We incorporate motivation with three variants of RL in Chap. 6.

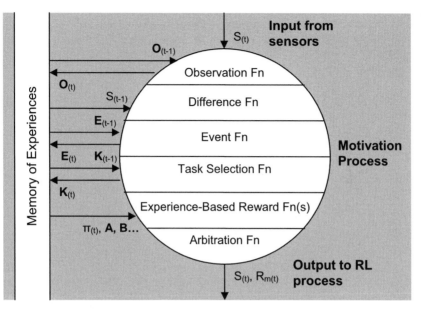

Fig. 5.7. Diagrammatic representation of motivation for attention focus.

5.3 Curiosity as Motivation for Support Characters

Laird and van Lent [10] identified the conversational and behavioural aspects of existing support characters as open research problems. Generating behaviours for support characters with an intrinsic motivation function responds to this challenge with an adaptive learning approach. Motivation is a process that uses observations and events to represent potentially motivating learning tasks, unsupervised learning algorithms for adaptive task selection, and mathematical models of psychological motivation theories to compute motivation values for tasks. In this section we trace two paths through this general model of motivation to create two models of curiosity for NPCs using interest and competency.

5.3.1 Curiosity as Interesting Events

Curiosity is a kind of motivation that is based on interesting events in the environment. A curious NPC will be able to respond to changes in the environment by shifting his attention to novel events and focus on behaviours that reinforce that change. This is a very different behaviour to many NPCs in which the programmed behaviour is predefined as a set of rules or actions that loop through the set of tasks known to the NPC. A model of motivation using interesting events is a starting point for modelling support characters that learn by trial-and-error to perform interesting achievement tasks based on the materials in their environment.

The first algorithm for motivation based on curiosity as interesting events is shown in Fig. 5.8. The algorithm begins in line 1 by computing events using Difference Function 3 from Table 5.2. The use of Difference Function 3 focuses attention on any change in the environment between one sensed state and the next, that is, any potentially motivating achievement task. Event Function 2 from Table 5.3 is used in line 2 to produce a single event that focuses attention on all potentially motivating achievement tasks. Task selection is achieved in line 3 using the modified SOM from Sect. 5.2.3 to identify a single task model representing the current event. Reward is then computed using the modified version of the Saunders [4] interest function. As there is only a single event and reward function, the interest value is used directly as the motivation signal, without arbitration. The model of motivation presented in this section, when combined with an appropriate learning algorithm from Chap. 6, offers a starting point for the development of support characters that can learn behaviours for interesting achievement tasks.

1. Subtract $S_{(t)} - S_{(t')}$ using

$$\Delta(s_{L(t)}, s_{L(t-1)}) = \begin{cases} s_{L(t)} & \text{if } \neg\exists\ s_{L(t')} \\ -s_{L(t')} & \text{if } \neg\exists\ s_{L(t)} \\ s_{L(t)} - s_{L(t')} & \text{if } s_{L(t)} - s_{L(t')} \neq 0 \\ \text{null} & \text{otherwise} \end{cases}$$

2. Compose $\mathbf{E}_{S(t)} = \{E_{(t)}\}$ where
   $E_{(t)} = (\Delta(s_{1(t)}, s_{1(t-1)}), \Delta(s_{2(t)}, s_{2(t-1)}), \ldots \Delta(s_{L(t)}, s_{L(t-1)}), \ldots)$
3. Distinguish $K_{(t)}$ using a SOM.
4. Compute $I(K_{(t)})$
5. Output $R_{m(t)} = I(K_{(t)})$

Fig. 5.8 Algorithmic description of motivation to achieve interesting events.

A key concern when combining models of motivation with RL algorithms is the sensitivity of the learning algorithm to the values of the parameters defining the motivation function. The interest function described above is defined by ten constants, summarised in Table 5.7, which affect the shape of the Wundt curve and thus the motivation value computed at each time-step. The habituation parameters τ_1, τ_2 and α govern the rate of change of the values stored in the neurons in the habituating layer. τ_1 governs the rate at which novelty decreases in habituating neurons connected to SOM neurons in the winning neighbourhood, while τ_2 governs the rate at which novelty increases in habituating neurons connected to losing SOM neurons. Marsland et al. suggest the values $\tau_1 = 3.3$ and $\tau_2 = 14.3$ [5]. These values are a good starting point for developing NPCs. Figure 5.9 shows that higher values of τ increase the number of times a stimulus can fire (or not fire) in order for novelty to reach its extreme values of 0 and 1. This property may be useful in complex environments where more time is required to learn complex tasks.

The parameter α determines the minimum possible novelty. In gaming applications it is appropriate for novelty to ranges between 0 and 1 to represent high and low familiarity with an event for input to the Wundt function. The value $\alpha = 1.05$ suggested by Marsland et al. [5] achieves this range as shown in Fig. 5.9. Values $\alpha < 1.0$ are inappropriate as they produce negative novelty values. In addition, Fig. 5.10 shows that values significantly higher than 1.05 are also inappropriate as novelty no longer achieves its full possible range. Such values would affect the range of interest values possible from the Wundt curve.

F_{max}^{+} and F_{max}^{-} are the maximum positive and negative reward values for novelty. As the motivation function described in this section uses interest directly as reward, in order to achieve a reward signal $0 \leq R \leq 1$, a value of 1 is appropriate for these parameters. ρ^{+} and ρ^{-} are the gradients of the sigmoid reward functions. Lower values of these variables produce more gradual growth and decay of interest than higher values as shown in Fig. 5.11. This affects the amount of time a task can receive the maximum interest value as a

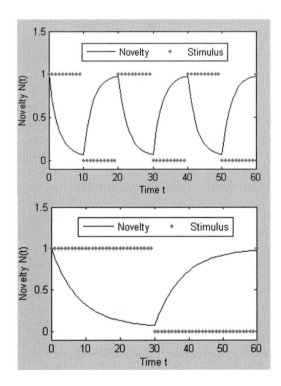

Fig. 5.9 Change in novelty with $\alpha = 1.05$ and **(a)** $\tau_1 = \tau_2 = 3.3$ and **(b)** $\tau_1 = \tau_2 = 9$.

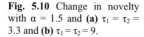
Fig. 5.10 Change in novelty with α = 1.5 and (**a**) $\tau_1 = \tau_2 = 3.3$ and (**b**) $\tau_1 = \tau_2 = 9$.

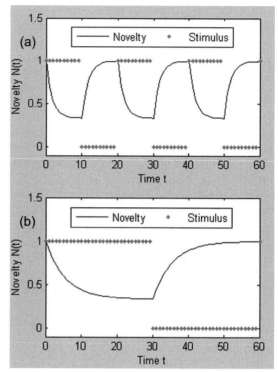

reward signal. F_{min}^+ and F_{min}^- are the turning points of the positive and negative reward functions. Adjustment of these values also affects the time a task can receive the maximum interest value as shown in Fig. 5.12.

We use moderate values for each interest parameter that produce a smooth increase and decrease in interest and that achieve interest values covering the full range of values between 0 and 1. The interest, RL and metric parameters used in all the experiments in this book are summarised in Table 5.7.

The simple, extrospective model of motivation presented in this section has potential for learning simple tasks in complex, dynamic environments. It is possible that learning will display some sensitivity to changes in parameters of the motivation function. For example, high values of τ_1 and τ_2 may improve behavioural complexity attained in environments with tasks requiring longer behavioural cycles. However, finding values for these parameters that achieve specific behavioural variety or complexity characteristics is likely to require careful tuning for any given environment. Other algorithms that modify the shape of the motivation curve while learning is in progress have the potential to avoid this problem. Such algorithms will use some form of introspection to allow the learning process to influence the motivation signal. Such a model is proposed in the next section.

Fig. 5.11 Change in interest with **(a)** $\rho^+ = \rho^- = 5$, $F_{min}^+ = 0.5$ and $F_{min}^- = 1.5$ and **(b)** $\rho^+ = \rho^- = 30$, $F_{min}^+ = 0.5$ and $F_{min}^- = 1.5$

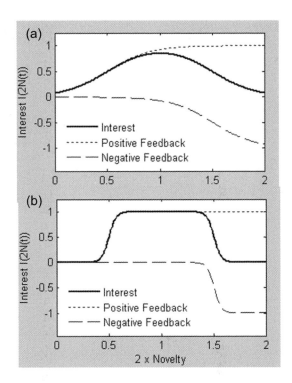

Table 5.7 Parameters and their values for motivated reinforcement learning agents motivated to achieve interesting events.

	Parameter	Value
Reinforcement Learning Parameters	γ	0.9
	β	0.9
	ε	0.1
	Φ_1 and Φ_3	0.8
	Φ_2	1000
Interest Parameters	η	0.1
	α	1.05
	τ_1	3.3
	τ_2	14.3
	F_{max}^+ and F_{max}^-	1
	ρ^+ and ρ^-	10
	F_{min}^+	0.5
	F_{min}^-	1.5
Metric Parameters	r	0.2
	h	20
	p	0.001

Fig. 5.12 Change in interest with **(a)** $\rho^+ = \rho^- = 10$, $F_{min}^+ = 0.1$ and $F_{min}^- = 1.9$ and **(b)** $\rho^+ = \rho^- = 10$, $F_{min}^+ = 0.9$ and $F_{min}^- = 1.1$

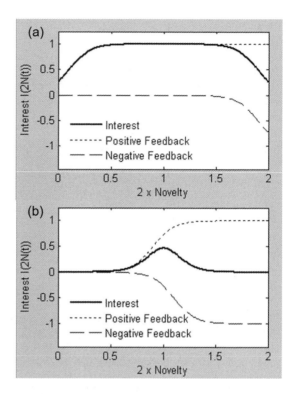

5.3.2   Curiosity as Interest and Competence

A model of motivation based purely on interest does not always allow the agent enough time to become competent at any task. Combining concepts of interest and competence presents a second kind of curiosity: one that allows the agent to be distracted by an interesting event when the value of being distracted is greater than the value of becoming competent at the current task.

The second algorithm for motivation based on interest and competence is shown in Fig. 5.13. In this algorithm, interest and competence compete to motivate learning. A computational model of interest is used to focus attention on new, interesting achievement tasks, while a computational model of competence competes to maintain the current focus of attention for long enough to ensure that a stable behavioural cycle containing that task has emerged.

The algorithm begins as for motivation using interesting events. In line 1 events are computed using Difference Function 3 from Table 5.2. The use of Difference Function 3 again focuses attention on any change in the environment between one sensed state and the next, that is, any potentially motivating achievement task. Event Function 2 from Table 5.3 is used in line 2 to produce a single event that focuses attention on all potentially motivating achievement tasks. Task selection is achieved in line 3 using the modified SOM to identify a single task model representing the current event. At this point the algorithm differs from the previous algorithm. A first motivation value is computed using the modified version of the Saunders [4] interest function. However, a second motivation value is computed using the model of competence motivation described in Chap. 2. These motivation values are combined using an arbitration function that represents competition between

```
1. Subtract S(t) - S(t') using

                      ⎧ s_L(t)   if ¬∃ s_L(t')
                      ⎪
   Δ(s_L(t), s_L(t-1)) = ⎨ -s_L(t')  if ¬∃ s_L(t)
                      ⎪
                      ⎪ s_L(t) - s_L(t')  if s_L(t) - s_L(t') ≠ 0
                      ⎩
                        null  otherwise

2. Compose E_S(t) = {E(t)} where
      E(t) = (Δ(s_1(t), s_1(t-1)), Δ(s_2(t), s_2(t-1)),...Δ(s_L(t), s_L(t-1)),...)
3. Distinguish K(t) using a SOM.
4. Repeat (for each R_j ∈ {I,C}):
5.      Compute R_j(K(t)) using the reward function R_j
6. Output R_m(t) = max(I(K(t)), C(K(t)))
```

Fig. 5.13 Algorithmic description of motivation using interest and competence.

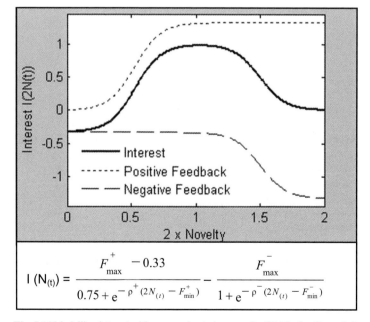

$$I(N_{(t)}) = \frac{F^+_{max} - 0.33}{0.75 + e^{-\rho^+(2N_{(t)} - F^+_{min})}} - \frac{F^-_{max}}{1 + e^{-\rho^-(2N_{(t)} - F^-_{min})}}$$

Fig. 5.14 Modelling interest with an aversion to low novelty (highly familiar tasks).

interest and competence motivation by maximising the output motivation
signal as shown in line 6.

The model of motivation presented in this section, when combined with an
appropriate MRL algorithm from Chap. 6, offers a potentially more scalable
model of motivation for support characters that can learn competent
behaviours for interesting achievement tasks. The same parameter values are
used for interest as in the previous algorithm and also for the corresponding
parameters in the competence model. However, in order to motivate the pursuit
of competence more strongly than the pursuit of interest, the shape of the
Wundt curve used to model interest is modified as shown in Fig. 5.14 to model
an aversion to highly familiar tasks. The interest, competence, RL and metric
parameters used in the experiments in the following chapters are summarised
in Table 5.8.

Table 5.8 Parameters and their values for motivated reinforcement learning agents motivated by interest and competence.

	Parameter	Value
Reinforcement Learning Parameters	γ	0.9
	β	0.9
	ε	0.1
	Φ_1 and Φ_3	0.8
	Φ_2	1000
Interest Parameters	η	0.1
	α	1.05
	τ_1	3.3
	τ_2	14.3
	F_{max}^{+} and F_{max}^{-}	1
	ρ^{+} and ρ^{-}	10
	F_{min}^{+}	0.5
	F_{min}^{-}	1.5
Competence Parameters	F_{max}^{+} and F_{max}^{-}	1
	ρ^{+} and ρ^{-}	10
	F_{min}^{+}	0.5
	F_{min}^{-}	1.5
Metric Parameters	r	0.2
	h	20
	p	0.001

5.4 Summary

In psychological theory, motivation has been attributed to a wide range of biological, cognitive and social forces that stimulate the emergence of biological, behavioural and social cycles. The mathematical models that describe these theories are thus a key component for achieving adaptive behavioural cycles in artificial systems. At the same time, existing RL algorithms are characterised by the use of a scalar reward signal that directs learning. To achieve compatibility between motivation theories and RL in order to build MRL algorithms, we have developed a mechanism that will identify and arbitrate over the motivation values produced by psychologically inspired mathematical models to produce a scalar motivation signal. We have selected interest and competence as the relevant types of motivation that will produce a curious learner. The next chapter shows how these models of motivation can be incorporated with different RL variants to achieve MRL agents capable of different types of behaviour.

5.5 References

[1] M. Wooldridge and N. Jennings, Intelligent agents: theory and practice. The Knowledge Engineering Review 10:115–152, 1995.

[2] A. Merceron, Languages and logic, Pearson Education Australia, 2001.

[3] S. Singh, A.G. Barto and N. Chentanez, Intrinsically motivated reinforcement learning, Advances in Neural Information Processing Systems (NIPS), 17:1281–1288, 2005.

[4] R. Saunders, Curious design agents and artificial creativity, Faculty of Architecture, University of Sydney, Sydney, 2001.

[5] S. Marsland, U. Nehmzow and J. Shapiro, A real-time novelty detector for a mobile robot, EUREL European Advanced Robotics Systems Masterclass and Conference, 2000.

[6] J.C. Stanley, Computer simulation of a model of habituation. Nature 261:146–148, 1976.

[7] R.W. White, Motivation reconsidered: The concept of competence. Psychological Review 66:297–333, 1959.

[8] E. Deci and R. Ryan, Intrinsic motivation and self-determination in human behavior, Plenum Press, New York, 1985.

[9] G.A. Carpenter and S. Grossberg, The ART of adaptive pattern recognition by a self-organizing neural network. IEEE Computer 21:77–88, 1988.

[10] J. Laird and M. van Lent, Interactive computer games: human-level AI's killer
       application, National Conference on Artificial Intelligence (AAAI), pp. 1171–
       1178, 2000.

Chapter 6
Motivated Reinforcement Learning Agents

Motivated reinforcement learning agents combine a model of motivation with a reinforcement learning algorithm. The output of the motivation function becomes the reward signal input for the reinforcement learning algorithm. In this chapter we begin by providing a general motivated reinforcement learning algorithm that assumes an understanding of the computational models of curiosity based on interest and competence presented in Chap. 5. We then develop this general model using three specific reinforcement learning approaches.

As seen in Chap. 3, there are many variations on reinforcement learning, where each one is suitable for a specific kind of learning environment. In the second part of this chapter, we combine our models of motivation with three different reinforcement learning algorithms: a flat reinforcement learning algorithm in which one policy is learned and adapted in response to the reward function; a multioption reinforcement learning algorithm in which a policy can have options that are stored and can be recalled; and a hierarchical learning algorithm in which a policy can be decomposed into a hierarchy of subpolicies that can be combined and reused to solve more complex problems. These three approaches can be thought of as different reasoning processes for creating non-player characters with different behavioural characteristics.

6.1 A General Motivated Reinforcement Learning Model

Our general motivated reinforcement learning (MRL) model uses continuing task, temporal difference (TD) learning and generalised policy iteration (GPI). Use of a continuing task model means that the agent reasons about an infinite experience trajectory. This is characteristic of lifelong learning, which is required of non-player characters (NPCs) in persistent virtual worlds. We use the TD learning approach as this class of reinforcement learning (RL) algorithm is fully incremental and can learn at each step of interaction with the

K.E. Merrick, M.L. Maher, *Motivated Reinforcement Learning*, DOI 10.1007/978-3-540-89187-1_6,
© Springer-Verlag Berlin Heidelberg 2009

environment without requiring distinct learning episodes. This is also important for achieving characters with realistic, lifelong learning. The key differences between the MRL algorithms in this chapter and existing TD learning algorithms described in Chap. 3 are:

- The reward function implements experience-based attention focus based on computational models of motivation.

- The state-action table or equivalent structure is initialised incrementally.

- The state and action spaces are implemented using a context free grammar (CFG).

Figure 6.1 shows our basic MRL control strategy for agent reasoning that achieves attention focus in the calculation of the reward function, followed by a policy update to adapt the agent's behaviour. The algorithm is arranged in five phases:

1. Sensing the environment (line 3): first the agent captures data from its sensors and associates this set of data with time t.

2. Policy improvement (lines 4–6): next the agent initialises its behaviour policy for the current state, if it has not been encountered before, and selects an action from the current policy.

3. Experience-based attention focus using motivation (lines 7–9): here the agent updates it experience trajectory and computes a reward signal using a motivation function.

4. Policy evaluation (line 10): the agent then modifies its policy to optimise for the expected reward.

5. Activation (line 12): finally the agent executes the selected action.

```
1.   Y(0) = Ø
2.   Repeat (forever):
3.       Sense S(t)
4.       if (Q(S(t), A) not initialised):
5.           initialise Q(S(t), A) arbitrarily ∀ A
6.       Choose A(t) from S(t) using the policy improvement fn
7.       Update Y(t)
8.       if (S(t-1) is initialised):
9.           Compute Rm(t)
10.          Update Q for S(t-1) and A(t-1) using policy eval fn
11.      S(t-1) ← S(t); A(t-1) ← A(t)
12.      Execute A(t)
```

Fig. 6.1 The motivated reinforcement learning algorithm uses a continuing task flow of control. Motivation is computed as an experience-based reward signal.

In summary, the MRL reward signal, defined by rules about the state space in reinforcement learning (RL), is replaced by a motivation signal computed based on experiences; and the state-action table or equivalent is initialised with sensed states and actions incrementally, since attention is focused in response to new experiences, rather than prior to learning. This means that the agent does not need to have prior knowledge of the state and action spaces. The structure of this algorithm allows either on-policy or off-policy TD control strategies to be used for policy evaluation and improvement without restructuring the underlying algorithm. Both these approaches are considered in the next section.

6.2 Algorithms for Motivated Reinforcement Learning

This section presents MRL algorithms that use the model of motivation from Chap. 5 for attention focus with RL. First we extend flat TD learning by introducing a motivation signal to replace the reward signal. For the remainder of this book, such models are distinguished from references to MRL in general, as motivated flat reinforcement learning (MFRL). We then extend MFRL with the ability to recall and reuse learned behaviours, using motivated multioption reinforcement learners (MMORL) and motivated hierarchical reinforcement learners (MHRL). The differences between MFRL, MMORL and MHRL are illustrated through the presentation of agent models that show how the motivation and learning processes interact. These agent models are demonstrated and compared in specific scenarios in Part III.

6.2.1 Motivated Flat Reinforcement Learning

Figure 6.2 expands the general model for MRL presented above for use with an off-policy TD control strategy, Q-learning. Fig. 6.3 expands the model for use with an on-policy control strategy, SARSA. In the context of NPCs, Q-learning can be thought of as the more aggressive learning approach, while SARSA results in NPCs with more cautious behavioural policies. Figure 6.4 shows diagrammatically how MFRL agents extend traditional RL agents by the addition of a motivation process that computes a motivation signal $R_{m(t)}$. Sensors monitor the world and return the sensed state as in line 3 of the algorithms in Figs. 6.2 and 6.3. The motivation process performs the algorithm from Chap. 5 in line 9. The RL process performs the initialisation of the state-action table or equivalent, policy improvement and policy evaluation functions. Finally the chosen action triggers an effector that causes a transition to occur in the world. This corresponds to line 12 in Figs. 6.2 and 6.3.

```
1.  Y(0) = ∅
2.  Repeat (forever):
3.        Sense S(t)
4.        if (Q(S(t), A) not initialised):
5.                    initialise Q(S(t), A) arbitrarily ∀ A
6.        A(t) = argmax f (Q(S(t), A))
                 A∈A
7.        Update Y(t)
8.        if (S(t-1) is initialised):
9.                 Compute Rm(t)
10.                Q(S(t-1), A(t-1)) ← Q(S(t-1), A(t-1))
                      + β[Rm(t) + γ max Q(S(t), A) - Q(S(t-1), A(t-1))]
                                    A∈A
11.       S(t-1) ← S(t); A(t-1) ← A(t)
12.       Execute A(t)
```

Fig. 6.2 The motivated Q-learning algorithm.

```
1.  Y(0) = ∅
2.  Repeat (forever):
3.        Sense S(t)
4.        if (Q(S(t), A) not initialised):
5.                    initialise Q(S(t), A) arbitrarily ∀ A
6.        A(t) = argmax f (Q (S(t), A))
                 A∈A
7.        Update Y(t)
8.        if (S(t-1) is initialised):
9.                 Compute Rm(t)
10.                Q(S(t-1), A(t-1)) ← Q(S(t-1), A(t-1))
                      + β[Rm(t) + γQ(S(t), A(t)) - Q(S(t-1), A(t-1))]
11.       S(t-1) ← S(t); A(t-1) ← A(t)
12.       Execute A(t)
```

Fig. 6.3 The motivated SARSA algorithm.

MFRL is characterised by a single learned policy π. This policy is non-stationary and adapts to represent different behavioural cycles at different times, with a learned task forgotten as new behavioural cycles emerge. This represents the most flexible form of MRL as the policy always focuses on the agent's most recent experiences so there is little chance of obsolete data being remembered. Such adaptive behaviour is an advantage in highly dynamic environments or in applications such as NPCs where the continued evolution of new behavioural cycles contributes to the personality of the character. However, in some applications it may be an advantage if learned policies can be recalled and reused. For example, if a task can become highly motivating on more than one occasion, it may be advantageous to be able to recall previous learning for that task. Recall in MRL using multioption [1] and hierarchical learning is considered in the following sections.

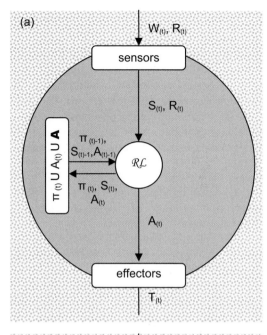

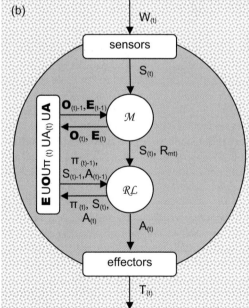

Fig. 6.4. Comparison of **(a)** flat reinforcement learning agents and **(b)** motivated flat reinforcement learning agents. Flat reinforcement learning agents take a reward signal from the environment, but motivated flat reinforcement learning agents incorporate a motivation process to compute an experience-based reward signal.

6.2.2 *Motivated Multioption Reinforcement Learning*

Previously, Saunders and Gero [2] achieved recall in a motivated agent setting using motivation to trigger preprogrammed reflexive behaviours. A reflex is an action or behaviour triggered when certain conditions about the current state of the environment or the agent are met [3]. For example, in the Saunders and Gero [2] model, interesting observations triggered preprogrammed behaviours such as walking towards the interesting stimulus. In this section, recall is implemented in a MRL setting by integrating motivated reflexes with option learning to create motivated, multioption reinforcement learning (MMORL). Rather than triggering preprogrammed behaviours, motivated reflexes trigger learned behavioural options. Learned knowledge is accumulated through the progressive creation of additional options representing the solution to individual tasks.

The option framework of Sutton et al. [4] is used to represent behavioural policies that become reflexive responses to high motivation. An option $B = \langle I, \pi, \Omega \rangle$ is a temporal abstraction that is initiated, takes control for some period of time and then eventually ends. $B.I$ is the initiation set of states in which the option applies, $B.\pi$ is the option policy that specifies what actions are executed for a subset of environment states and $B.\Omega$ is the termination function that specifies the conditions under which the option terminates. $B.\Omega(S_{(t)}) \rightarrow [0, 1]$ defines the probability with which the behavioural option B will terminate in the state $S_{(t)}$. Various multioption RL algorithms exist that progressively extend the action set **A** with a set **B** of behavioural options. While these algorithms have different purposes, the primary aim of the algorithm presented here is to facilitate recall for NPCs within a MRL setting.

In MMORL, each behavioural option B has an associated task model $B.K$ representing the task about which it is to accumulate knowledge. Behavioural options themselves undergo policy improvement and evaluation, using the set **A** of actions to construct the policy $B.\pi$. Each option has an associated memory of the previous action $B.A$ selected by the policy improvement function. A summary of the structures associated with a behavioural option for MMORL is given in Table 6.1.

The previous section modelled MFRL for Q-learning and SARSA in five phases concerned with sensing the environment, policy improvement, experience-based attention focus using motivation, policy evaluation and activation. This section extends the MFRL algorithm for Q-learning to multioption learning. The key differences between the MFRL algorithm in the previous section and MMORL algorithm shown in Fig. 6.5 are the addition of a sixth phase for reflexes controlling the addition and removal of behavioural policies (lines 8–12) and the expansion of the policy improvement and evaluation equations to the multioption learning setting (lines 13–24 and 28–31 respectively).

```
1.    Y(0) = ∅
2.    Repeat (forever):
3.        Sense S(t)
4.        if (Q(S(t), B) not initialised):
5.            initialise Q(S(t), B) arbitrarily ∀ B
6.        if (QB(S(t), A) not initialised for any B):
7.            initialise QB(S(t), A) arbitrarily ∀ A
8.        if (Rm(t) > Φ1):
9.            Repeat (for each K ∈ KS(t)):
10.               B(t) = B(t-1) + BK(t)
11.           if (B(t-1) ∉ A and B(t-1).τ > Φ2):
12.               B(t) = B(t-1) - B(t-1)
13.           if (B(t-1) ∈ A or B(t-1).Ω(S(t-1)) = 1):
14.               if (Rm(t) > Φ3 and ∃ B for K(t) and B.τ < Φ2):
15.                   B(t) = B
16.               else:
17.                   B(t) = argmax f(Q(S(t), B))
                            B∈B
18.       else:
19.           B(t) = B(t-1)
20.       if (B(t) ∉ A):
21.           A(t) = argmax f(QB(t)(S(t), A))
                        A∈A
22.           B(t).A ← A(t)
23.       else:
24.           A(t) = B(t)
25.       Update Y(t)
26.       if (S(t-1) is initialised):
27.           Compute Rm(t)
28.           if (B(t-1) ∈ A or B(t-1).Ω(S(t-1)) = 1):
29.               Q(S(t-1), B(t-1)) ← Q(S(t-1), B(t-1))
                      + β[Rm(t) + γ max Q(S(t), B) - Q(S(t-1), B(t-1))]
                               B∈B
30.           if (B(t-1) ∉ A):
31.               QB(t-1)(S(t-1), B(t-1).A) ← QB(t-1)(S(t-1), B(t-1).A) +
                      β[B(t-1).Ω(S(t-1)) + γ max QB(t-1)(S(t), A) -
                                           A∈A
                      QB(t-1)(S(t-1), B(t-1).A)]
32.               if (B(t-1).Ω(S(t-1)) = 1):
33.                   B(t-1).τ = 0
34.               else:
35.                   B(t-1).τ = B(t-1).τ + 1
36.       S(t-1) ← S(t); B(t-1) ← B(t)
37.       Execute A(t)
```

Fig. 6.5 The motivated, multioption Q-learning algorithm.

Table 6.1 Structures associated with behavioural options in motivated, multioption reinforcement learning.

Structure	Description	Note
$B.I$	Initiation set	Precup et al.'s [1]
$B.\pi$	Option policy	original option
$B.\Omega$	Termination function	framework.
$B.K$	Task to learn	Additional
$B.A$	Last action selected by this option	structures for
$B.\tau$	Number of actions selected by this option since the last occurrence of $B.K$	MMORL.

The MMORL model incorporates three reflexes for creating, disabling and triggering behavioural options. New behavioural options are created (lines 8–10) when tasks with a motivation value greater than a threshold Φ_1 are encountered. The reverse process in which options are removed from the set $\mathbf{B}_{(t-1)}$ is often omitted from multioption or hierarchical RL models. However, option removal becomes important in dynamic environments where tasks that were once highly motivating can cease to occur. In such cases, the termination condition of some behavioural options may be impossible to fulfil. When the learning agent initiates such an option it will continue to search for a policy for a task that can no longer be achieved. In our algorithm, a time-based reflex (lines 11–12) is employed in which options are temporarily disabled if their termination condition has not been met for a period longer than Φ_2. If the task that triggered the creation of the option achieves a motivation value greater than a threshold Φ_1 once more, the option is re-enabled with a larger value of Φ_2. A summary of the reflexes is provided in Table 6.2.

Table 6.2 Reflex rules used in motivated, multioption reinforcement learning.

Rule	Description
If $R_{m(t)}$ is greater than Φ_1 then create a new behavioural option B for the current task $K_{(t)}$.	Rule defining when to create new behavioural options.
If $B.\tau$ is greater than Φ_2 then disable the behavioural option B.	Rule defining when to disable existing behavioural options.
If $R_{m(t)}$ is greater than Φ_3 then trigger the reflex behaviour B for which $B.K$ corresponds to the current highly motivating task K.	Rule defining when to trigger existing behavioural options.

In the multioption setting, the policy evaluation equation (lines 28–31) becomes a two-step process. When the current behavioural option is a primitive action or in a terminal state, the standard Q-learning update is applied (line 29). However, when the current behavioural option is mid-policy an additional learning update is made using the termination function as the reward signal for the option (line 31). The termination function $B_{(t)}.\Omega$ returns a result of 1 when a task model from $\mathbf{K}_{S(t)}$ matches the task model $B.K$ that originally triggered the creation of the option $B_{(t)}$ and 0 otherwise, as follows:

$$B_{(t)}.\Omega(S_{(t)}) = \begin{cases} 1 \text{ if } B.K \in \mathbf{K}_{S(t)} \\ 0 \text{ otherwise} \end{cases}$$

Using this termination function, behavioural options are rewarded most highly when they achieve the task they were created to represent.

Figure 6.6 shows diagrammatically how MMORL agents extend MFRL agents by the addition of a reflex process that manages the creation, removal and triggering of behavioural options. Sensors monitor the world and return the sensed state as in line 2 of the algorithms in Fig. 6.5. The motivation process represents the algorithm in Chap. 5 in line 27 in Fig. 6.5. The reflex process represents lines 8–15 of the algorithm in Fig. 6.5. The MORL process represents the initialisation of the state-action table or equivalent, policy improvement in lines 17–24 and policy evaluations functions in lines 28–31. Finally the chosen action triggers an effector that causes a transition to occur in the world. This corresponds to line 37 in Fig. 6.5.

MMORL is characterised by a two-level hierarchy in which the parent policy π defines adaptive behavioural cycles and the child policies $B.\pi$ encapsulate cycles for individual tasks. This extends MFRL with the ability to accumulate knowledge for a task that becomes highly motivating more than once. This is important for the design of NPCs in environments where tasks may occur repeatedly, but separated by some time period. It means that the NPC need not relearn its behavioural cycle for the task, but can simply recall and execute an appropriate stored behavioural policy.

In the general option framework, options can invoke other options as actions, thus making it possible for behaviours to have a multi-level hierarchical structure. This allows existing behavioural options to be used while learning new behavioural options and can speed learning. Recall and reuse with multi-layer hierarchies are considered in the MHRL algorithm in the next section.

Fig. 6.6 Comparison of **(a)** motivated flat reinforcement learning agents and **(b)** motivated, multi-option reinforcement learning agents. Motivated, multi-option reinforcement learning agents incorporate a reflex process to create, remove and trigger behavioural options

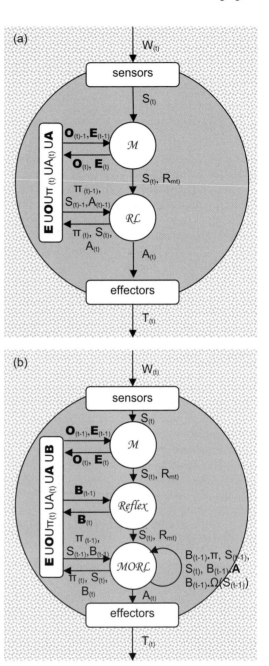

6.2.3 Motivated Hierarchical Reinforcement Learning

The previous section modelled MMORL for Q-learning in six phases concerned with sensing the environment, reflexes for creating, removing and triggering behavioural options, policy improvement, experience-based attention focus using motivation, policy evaluation and activation. In this section the MMORL algorithm for Q-learning is extended to hierarchical learning. The key difference between the MMORL algorithm in the previous section and the MHRL algorithm – shown in Fig. 6.8 below – is the further expansion of the policy improvement and evaluation equations (lines 14–26 and 30–35 below, respectively) to the hierarchical setting.

The ability to reuse recalled behavioural options extends MMORL with the ability to abstract learned behavioural options. This can speed-up learning if behavioural options are chosen appropriately. In MRL, faster learning translates to faster adaptation in dynamic environments and more rapid acquisition of policies for multiple tasks in complex environments. MHRL agents have a similar structure to MMORL agents, with processes for motivation, reflexes and HRL. The MHRL agent model is shown in Fig. 6.7.

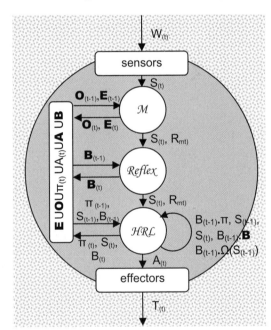

Fig. 6.7 The motivated hierarchical reinforcement learning agent model.

```
1.   Y(0) = ∅
2.   Repeat (forever):
3.       Sense S(t)
4.       if (Q(S(t), B) not initialised):
5.           initialise Q(S(t), B) arbitrarily ∀B
6.       if (QB(S(t), B) not initialised for any B):
7.           initialise QB(S(t), B) arbitrarily ∀B in B.B
8.       if (Rm(t) > Φ1):
9.           Repeat (for each K ∈ KS(t)):
10.              B(t) = B(t-1) + BK(t)

11.              BK(t).B = B(t-1)

12.       if (B(t-1) ∉ A and B(t-1).τ > Φ3):
13.           B(t) = B(t-1) - B(t-1)
14.       if (B(t-1) ∈ A or B(t-1).Ω(S(t-1)) = 1):
15.           if (Rm(t) > Φ3 and ∃B for K(t) and B.τ < Φ2):
16.               B(t) = B
17.           else:
18.               B(t) = argmax f (Q (S(t), B))
                          B∈B
19.       else:
20.           B(t) = B(t-1)
21.       B = B(t)
22.       Repeat (while B ∉ A):
23.           Bb = argmax f (Q B(S(t), B))
                      B∈B
24.           B.B = Bb
25.           B = Bb
26.       A(t) = B
27.       Update Y(t)
28.       if (S(t-1) is initialised):
29.           Compute Rm(t)
30.           if (B(t-1) ∈ A or B(t-1).Ω(S(t-1)) = 1):
31.               Q(S(t-1), B(t-1)) ← Q(S(t-1), B(t-1)) + β[Rm(t) +
                       γ max Q(S(t), B)  - Q(S(t-1), B(t-1))]
                        B∈B
32.           B = B(t-1)
33.           Repeat (while B ∉ A):
34.               B.Rc = B.Rc + γ^(B.τ) B.Ω(S(t-1)); B.τ = B.τ + 1;
35.               QB(S(t-1),B.B) ← QB(S(t-1),B.B)+
                       β[B.Rc+γ^(B.τ) max QB(S(t),B) - QB(S(t-1),B.B)]
                               B∈B.B
36.               if (B.Ω(S(t-1)) = 1):
37.                   B.Rc = 0; B.τ = 0;
38.               B = B.B
39.       S(t-1) ← S(t); B(t-1) ← B(t)
40.       Execute A(t)
```

Fig. 6.8 The motivated hierarchical Q-learning algorithm.

In MHRL, behavioural options are improved and evaluated, reasoning about a set **B** of other behavioural options. These must be chosen to ensure the behavioural hierarchy does not contain cycles. Each behavioural option has associated memory of the previous option $B.B$ selected by the option and the cumulative reward $B.R_c$ generated while subbehaviours are executing. A summary of the structures associated with a behavioural option for MHRL is given in Table 6.3.

Table 6.3 Structures associated with behavioural options in motivated hierarchical reinforcement learning.

Structure	Description	Note
$B.I$	Initiation set	Precup et al.'s
$B.\pi$	Option policy	original option
$B.\Omega$	Termination function	framework.
$B.K$	Task to learn	
$B.B$	Last option selected by this option	
$B.\tau$	Number of actions selected by this option since the last occurrence of $B.K$	Additional structures for
$B.R_c$	Cumulative reward	MHRL.
$B.\mathbf{B}$	Possible options (including primitive actions) that can be selected by this option	

6.3 Summary

The algorithms in this chapter incorporate the model of motivation for attention focus from Chap. 5 with different RL approaches. The first two MFRL algorithms extend existing TD learning approaches by introducing a motivation signal to replace the reward signal. These algorithms can be used to create NPCs that are either cautious or aggressive in their learning.

The third and fourth algorithms extend MFRL with the ability to recall and reuse learned behaviours, respectively. Recall is achieved in a MRL setting by integrating the motivated reflex response used by Saunders and Gero [2] to an option learning setting. Three reflexes are considered for creating, removing and triggering learned behavioural options. The idea of removing or temporarily inactivating learned behavioural options is important for agents in dynamic environments. Agents that cannot forget learned behavioural options risk focusing attention on tasks that are no longer relevant after an environmental change.

The use of reflexes to trigger important processes does have some limitations. The decision thresholds that define when reflexes fire, for example, must be fixed prior to interaction with the environment. Furthermore, values for decision thresholds that ensure good performance may also depend on the motivation component used and the range and distribution of the motivation signal. While this can be known in advance to some extent, the exact operational range may depend on environmental factors.

The notion of incorporating recall in a MRL setting is important for certain NPCs where the ability to recall previous learning is an advantage. However, recall has the potential disadvantage that obsolete data may be stored, making adaptation more difficult in dynamic environments. In addition, the use of the termination function to direct learning at the option level in the MMORL and MHRL models reduces the time that motivation directs learning. This also has the potential to affect the adaptability and multitask learning ability of these agents. These issues and their impact on the emergent behaviour of NPCs are considered with respect to specific scenarios in the studies in Part III.

6.4 References

[1] D. Precup, R. Sutton and S. Singh, Theoretical results on reinforcement learning with temporally abstract options, The 10th European Conference on Machine Learning, Chemnitz, Germany, Springer Verlag, pp. 382–393, 1998.

[2] R. Saunders and J.S. Gero, Curious agents and situated design evaluations. In: J.S. Gero and F.M.T. Brazier (Eds.), Agents in Design, Key Centre of Design Computing and Cognition, University of Sydney, pp. 133–149, 2002.

[3] M.L. Maher and J.S. Gero, Agent models of 3D virtual worlds, ACADIA 2002: Thresholds, California State Polytechnic University, Pamona, pp. 127–138, 2002.

[4] R. Sutton, D. Precup and S. Singh, Between MDPs and semi-MDPs: A framework for temporal abstraction in reinforcement learning. Artificial Intelligence 112:181–211, 1998.

Part III
Curious Characters in Games

Chapter 7
Curious Characters for Multiuser Games

Massively multiplayer online role-playing games (MMORPGs) are played in complex, persistent virtual worlds. Over time, the landscape of these worlds evolves and changes as players create and personalise their own virtual property. However, many existing approaches to the design of the non-player characters that populate virtual game worlds result in characters with a fixed set of preprogrammed behaviours. Such characters lack the ability to adapt and evolve in time with their surroundings. In addition, different characters must be individually programmed with different behaviours. Motivated reinforcement learning offers an alternative approach that achieves more adaptive characters. A game world can be populated with characters that use the same agent model, but which develop different behaviours over time based on their individual experiences in the world.

The focus of this chapter is on demonstrating motivated reinforcement learning for generating behaviours of non-player characters in a small-scale, isolated game scenario. Isolating game scenarios gives game designers greater control over the behaviour of non-player characters as each character is confined to a certain area. In the context of a large, complex virtual world, game locations are frequently isolated by terrain conditions, levelling requirements, or because non-player characters lack the sensory mechanisms to reason about events beyond their immediate location. In this chapter we use a simple village setting as an example of a small-scale, isolated game scenario. However, other examples might include characters in a building, on a farm or in an underground dungeon. The next chapter considers larger-scale settings in which characters have greater freedom to move to more locations and perform more complex tasks.

This chapter compares six different types of motivated reinforcement learning agents for controlling non-player characters. The different agents are developed by combining the models of motivation and learning from Part II. The metrics from Chap. 4 are used to provide an initial demonstration and

K.E. Merrick, M.L. Maher, *Motivated Reinforcement Learning*, DOI 10.1007/978-3-540-89187-1_7,
© Springer-Verlag Berlin Heidelberg 2009

evaluation of these models for controlling the behaviour of characters in the simulated village scenario.

7.1 Motivated Reinforcement Learning for Support Characters in Massively Multiplayer Online Role-Playing Games

The environment used in this experiment is a simulated role-playing game scenario, modelled on the village shown in Fig. 7.1. The village consists of two shops: a blacksmith's shop and a carpenter's shop. In addition, there is an iron mine and a forest nearby. A number of tools of these trades are available for non-player characters (NPCs) to pick up and use.

Formally, the village can be modelled as a set of two Markov decision processes (MDPs), P_1 and P_2, describing two regions of the village, one containing the objects required to mine iron-ore and forge weapons and another containing the objects required to cut timber and craft furniture. These regions can be described by the context-free grammar (CFG) in Fig. 7.2. This grammar describes the two regions P_1 and P_2 in terms of the locations, inventory and visible objects they support. Locations have enumerated values while visible objects and inventory are valued according to the number of units currently visible or held in inventory.

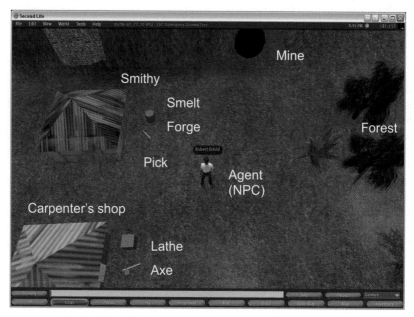

Fig. 7.1 A visualisation of the simulated game scenario in *Second Life*.

```
S                         →    <sensations>
<sensations>              →    <P₁Sensations><P₂Sensations>
<P₁Sensations>            →    <P₁location><P₁inventory><P₁visibleObjects>
<P₁location>              →    <mine> | <smithy>
<mine>                    →    1
<smithy>                  →    2
<P₁inventory>             →    <P₁objects>
<P₁visibleObjects>        →    <P₁objects>
<P₁objects>               →    <P₁object><P₁objects> | ε
<P₁object>                →    <pick> | <forge> | <smelt> | <iron-ore> |
                               <iron> | <weapons>
<P₂Sensations>            →    <P₂location><P₂inventory><P₂visibleObjects>
<P₂location>              →    <forest> | <carpenter-shop>
<forest>                  →    3
<carpenter-shop>          →    4
<P₂inventory>             →    <P₂objects>
<P₂visibleObjects>        →    <P₂objects>
<P₂objects>               →    <P₂object><P₂objects> | ε
<P₂object>                →    <axe> | <lathe> | <timber> |<furniture>
<pick>                    →    1
<forge>                   →    1
<smelt>                   →    1
<iron-ore>                →    1
<iron>                    →    1
<weapons>                 →    1
<axe>                     →    1
<lathe>                   →    1
<timber>                  →    1
<furniture>               →    1
```

Fig. 7.2 A context-free grammar for sensed states in a game scenario in which agents control non-player characters. Agents have location sensors, inventory sensors and object sensors.

The NPCs initially have no knowledge of the environment dynamics or how the different tools work. When they first encounter the environment they are equipped only with an empty backpack representing their inventory. In the game scenarios in this chapter the maximum number of any object that a NPC can hold in its inventory is one. The next chapter will explore the behaviour of motivated reinforcement learning (MRL) agents controlling NPCs in more complex environments with more MDPs, more complex MDPs, and environments where the set of regions **P** can change while NPCs are learning.

Some example sensed states in the environment used in this chapter are shown in label-sensation ($L{:}s$) format below. Labels L are constructed from the set of grammar variables while values for sensations come from the set of terminals.

```
S₍₁₎ ((location:2)(visiblePick:1)(visibleForge:1))
S₍₂₎ ((location:2)(inventoryPick:1)(visibleForge:1))
S₍₃₎ ((location:4)(inventoryPick:1)(visibleAxe:1)(visibleLathe:1))
```

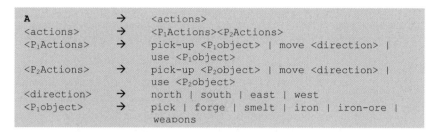

Fig. 7.3. A context-free grammar for the action set in a game environment in which agents have location effectors, pick-up object effectors and use object effectors.

NPCs can use the actions defined by the CFG in Fig. 7.3 to interact with their environment.

Possible tasks in this environment include travelling from place to place, cutting timber, mining iron-ore, smelting the ore to obtain iron, forging weapons and crafting furniture. Not all actions are available in all world states. Use actions are only available for a particular object if that object is in the current <inventory> or <visibleObjects> list of the agent. For example, it is appropriate to pick-up an axe and have it in inventory for later use, but the forge, which is too heavy to be picked up, can be used when it is visible. Move actions are available in any world state. Move actions change the <location> of the agent. Use actions change the <inventory> of an agent. For example, using the axe in the forest will result in the addition of timber to the agent's inventory and using the lathe will result in the removal of timber from the agent's inventory. A use action produces the desired result – such as addition of iron-ore to the agent's inventory when using the pick – 90% of the time and no result 10% of the time. Pick-up actions are only available for a particular object if that object is in the current <visibleObjects> list of the agent, that is, if the object and the agent are at the same location. Objects that can be picked up are added to the agent's <inventory>.

The actions that would produce the state sequence shown above are A(pick-up, pick) and A(move, east). The events produced by these actions are shown below. Each of these events represents a potentially motivating achievement task.

$E_{(1)}$ ((inventoryPick:1)(visiblePick:-1))
$E_{(2)}$ ((location:2)(visibleForge:-1)(visibleAxe:1)(visibleLathe:1))

The environment used in this demonstration has 52 states and 24 actions available across different states. This game environment is implemented as a *Java* simulation that can also be connected to the *Second Life* [1] virtual environment using XML-RPC to communicate sensations and actions between the agent program and the virtual world [2].

7.2 Character Behaviour in Small-Scale, Isolated Game Locations

This section compares the behaviour of NPCs using different MRL approaches. Six different types of MRL agent models are compared, differing in the motivation and learning components they use. Two different approaches to motivation are compared: motivation to achieve interesting events as described in Sect. 5.3.1 and motivation by interest and competence as described in Sect. 5.3.2. Each of these approaches is compared in the three learning settings described in Chap. 6: MFRL in which one behaviour is adapted by rewarding interesting tasks, MMORL in which new behaviours are generated and learned behaviours can be recalled, and MHRL in which new behaviours are generated and learned behaviours can be both recalled and reused. The six types of agent models are:

- ADAPT_INTEREST: A MFRL agent motivated to achieve interesting events;

- ADAPT_COMPETENCE: A MFRL agent motivated by interest and competence;

- RECALL_INTEREST: A MMORL agent motivated to achieve interesting events;

- RECALL_COMPETENCE: A MMORL agent motivated by interest and competence;

- REUSE_INTEREST: A MHRL agent motivated to achieve interesting events;

- REUSE_COMPETENCE: A MHRL agent motivated by interest and competence.

In Sect. 7.2.1 we begin by studying the behaviour of the simplest agents using the ADAPT_INTEREST model. Three of these agents are studied over a period of 50,000 time-steps in the environment described in the previous section. This provides a baseline against which we can understand the behaviour of agents using the other models. In Sect. 7.2.2 we present a more general comparison of the behaviour of agents using all six models. Agents using each of the models were run twenty times, again for 50,000 time-steps. The actions of each agent were logged and a statistical analysis of their behaviour made using the metrics from Chap. 4.

7.2.1   Case Studies of Individual Characters

Figure 7.4 illustrates behavioural cycles displayed by an ADAPT_INTEREST agent. Figure 7.4(a) shows a snapshot taken at t = 1,645, that is, after the agent had performed 1,645 actions in the environment. At this time, the agent is motivated to perform a travelling behaviour between the different locations in the environment. Figure 7.4(b) shows a second emergent behaviour at time t = 2,965. At this time, the same agent is motivated to move between four locations, use its axe to cut timber and use the lathe to make furniture. The cyclic behaviour evident in these snapshots represent a key result for MRL as it shows that structured, multitask learning can emerge from learning directed by a task independent model of curiosity. While the agent is not following an optimal policy for making furniture or cutting timber, its behaviour represents an optimal response to the current motivation signal.

The ability of the agent to transition from one behaviour to another is important for support characters, which have formerly suffered from fixed, repetitive behavioural sequences. Figure 7.4(c) shows a third behavioural cycle based on a snapshot at time t = 3,649. At this time, the agent is motivated to move between two locations, the mine and the blacksmith's shop, use its pick to mine iron ore, the smelt to extract iron and the forge to make weapons. This represents an optimal policy for repeating the weapons making task.

Figure 7.5 illustrates how agents using the same MRL model can develop different focuses of attention, and thus different characters, based on their experiences. Figure 7.5 shows the proportion of time devoted to different tasks in the game environment by two ADAPT_INTEREST agents. The first agent focuses its attention primarily on tasks concerned with forging weapons (E_1–E_5): mining iron-ore, smelting iron, travelling between the mine and the smithy and actually forging weapons. The second agent focuses primarily on tasks concerned with crafting furniture (E_8, E_{11}–E_{13}): cutting timber, travelling between the forest and the carpenter and using the lathe. Thus, the first agent has developed as a blacksmith character while the second has developed as a carpenter character. The ability of different agents to focus attention on different subsets of tasks based on their experiences in their environment is a key emergent property of MRL agents. In applications such as MMORPGs, a number of agents using identical agent models can learn different behavioural cycles, representing different characters. This removes the need for different rule sets of states to be hand crafted for different characters as is the case using the traditional reflex agent approach.

Anecdotally, the behavioural cycles learned by agents using the other five models showed similar structure to those learned by the ADAPT_INTEREST agents. However closer inspection reveals that the rate at which this behaviour is learned varies between models. This can be seen in the results in the next section.

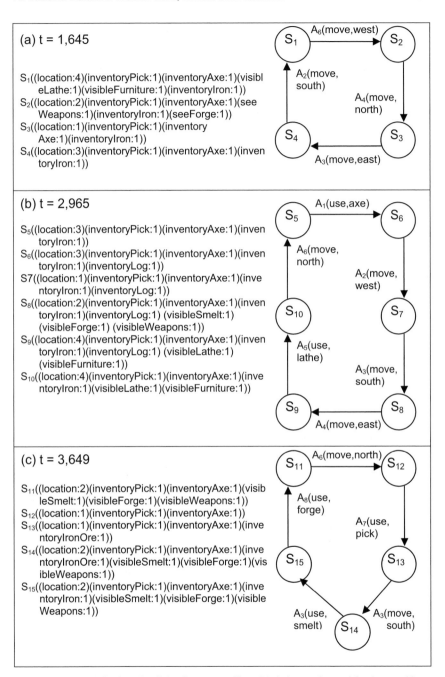

(a) t = 1,645

S_1((location:4)(inventoryPick:1)(inventoryAxe:1)(visibleLathe:1)(visibleFurniture:1)(inventoryIron:1))
S_2((location:2)(inventoryPick:1)(inventoryAxe:1)(seeWeapons:1)(inventoryIron:1)(seeForge:1))
S_3((location:1)(inventoryPick:1)(inventoryAxe:1)(inventoryIron:1))
S_4((location:3)(inventoryPick:1)(inventoryAxe:1)(inventoryIron:1))

(b) t = 2,965

S_5((location:3)(inventoryPick:1)(inventoryAxe:1)(inventoryIron:1))
S_6((location:3)(inventoryPick:1)(inventoryAxe:1)(inventoryIron:1)(inventoryLog:1))
$S7$((location:1)(inventoryPick:1)(inventoryAxe:1)(inventoryIron:1)(inventoryLog:1))
S_8((location:2)(inventoryPick:1)(inventoryAxe:1)(inventoryIron:1)(inventoryLog:1) (visibleSmelt:1) (visibleForge:1) (visibleWeapons:1))
S_9((location:4)(inventoryPick:1)(inventoryAxe:1)(inventoryIron:1)(inventoryLog:1) (visibleLathe:1) (visibleFurniture:1))
S_{10}((location:4)(inventoryPick:1)(inventoryAxe:1)(inventoryIron:1)(visibleLathe:1)(visibleFurniture:1))

(c) t = 3,649

S_{11}((location:2)(inventoryPick:1)(inventoryAxe:1)(visibleSmelt:1)(visibleForge:1)(visibleWeapons:1))
S_{12}((location:1)(inventoryPick:1)(inventoryAxe:1))
S_{13}((location:1)(inventoryPick:1)(inventoryAxe:1)(inventoryIronOre:1))
S_{14}((location:2)(inventoryPick:1)(inventoryAxe:1)(inventoryIronOre:1)(visibleSmelt:1)(visibleForge:1)(visibleWeapons:1))
S_{15}((location:2)(inventoryPick:1)(inventoryAxe:1)(inventoryIron:1)(visibleSmelt:1)(visibleForge:1)(visibleWeapons:1))

Fig. 7.4 Emergent behavioural policies for **(a)** travelling, **(b)** timber cutting and furniture making and **(c)** iron mining and weapons-smithing.

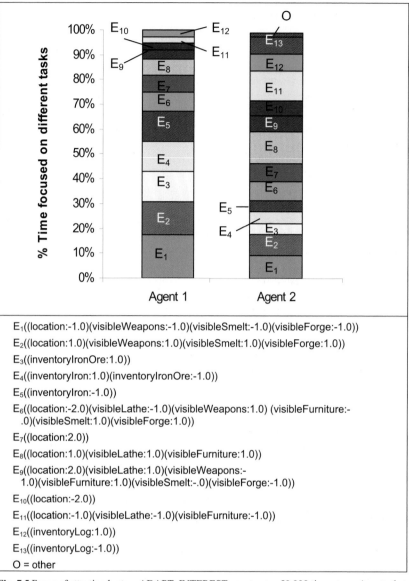

E_1((location:-1.0)(visibleWeapons:-1.0)(visibleSmelt:-1.0)(visibleForge:-1.0))

E_2((location:1.0)(visibleWeapons:1.0)(visibleSmelt:1.0)(visibleForge:1.0))

E_3((inventoryIronOre:1.0))

E_4((inventoryIron:1.0)(inventoryIronOre:-1.0))

E_5((inventoryIron:-1.0))

E_6((location:-2.0)(visibleLathe:-1.0)(visibleWeapons:1.0) (visibleFurniture:-.0)(visibleSmelt:1.0)(visibleForge:1.0))

E_7((location:2.0))

E_8((location:1.0)(visibleLathe:1.0)(visibleFurniture:1.0))

E_9((location:2.0)(visibleLathe:1.0)(visibleWeapons:-1.0)(visibleFurniture:1.0)(visibleSmelt:-.0)(visibleForge:-1.0))

E_10((location:-2.0))

E_11((location:-1.0)(visibleLathe:-1.0)(visibleFurniture:-1.0))

E_12((inventoryLog:1.0))

E_13((inventoryLog:-1.0))

O = other

Fig. 7.5 Focus of attention by two ADAPT_INTEREST agents over 50,000 time-steps. Agents that focus attention differently represent different game characters.

7.2.2   *General Trends in Character Behaviour*

Figure 7.6 compares the multitask learning ability of the different types of agents in terms of the behavioural variety achieved over a period of 50,000 time-steps. Error bars show the 95% confidence interval. The ADAPT_INTEREST and ADAPT_COMPETENCE agents display similar behavioural variety over this period, learning between seventeen and nineteen different behavioural cycles. In contrast, RECALL_INTEREST and RECALL_COMPETENCE agents learn between six and twelve behavioural cycles. Likewise, REUSE_INTEREST and REUSE_COMPETENCE agents learn between seven and twelve behavioural cycles. These statistics show that agents using all of the models are able to achieve multitask learning, but the ADAPT agents using MFRL learn more behavioural cycles in the same period.

The lower behavioural variety of the RECALL and REUSE agents is due to a reduction in the number of time-steps at which motivation values direct learning in MMORL and MHRL. In MMORL and MHRL, option learning is initiated by motivation, but directed at an option level by the termination function. The termination function is a binary function that assigns a reward of one each time the task that originally triggered the creation of an option is achieved and zero otherwise. In contrast the motivation functions directing learning in the MFRL setting have continuous valued outputs and frequently reward related tasks simultaneously. This can be seen in Table 7.1. The motivation function rewards all actions related to smelting iron highly, including using the pick to mine iron-ore and moving between the mine and the smithy.

The ability to reward related tasks simultaneously is a property of the interest function that emerges as a result of the natural juxtaposition of related tasks in an agent's experience trajectory. In contrast, the termination function only rewards the final act of smelting iron. This is also evident in Table 7.1.

Table 7.1 Comparison of reward from interest based motivation and a termination function.

Time	Action	Motivation to achieve interesting events	Termination Function
6639	A(use, smelt)	0.961563	1
6640	A(move, north)	0.935992	0
6641	A(use, pick)	0.953195	0
6642	A(move, south)	0.896915	0
6643	A(use, forge)	0.983858	0
6644	A(use, smelt)	0.953195	1
6645	A(move, north)	0.939472	0

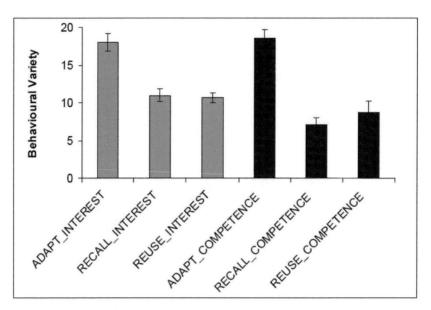

Fig. 7.6. Average behavioural variety achieved by the six different agent models.

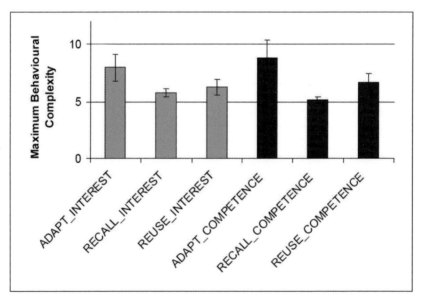

Fig. 7.7 Average maximum behavioural complexity achieved by the six different agent models.

Figure 7.7 characterises the multitask learning ability of the different types of agent in terms of their maximum behavioural complexity. In this game environment, the most complex single task is weapons making, which requires at least a five action behavioural cycle. This is shown as a grid line in Fig. 7.7. All agents achieve behavioural complexity significantly greater than five during the first 50,000 time-steps of their life. This indicates that they have the capacity to solve the most complex task in this small environment. ADAPT_INTEREST and ADAPT_COMPETENCE agents again show characteristically similar behaviour, learning behavioural cycles of significantly greater than five actions. This shows that they can interleave the solutions to multiple tasks in a single behavioural cycle. This is because the motivation functions can provide reward for more than one task during the same time period.

The RECALL_INTEREST and RECALL_COMPETNCE agents achieve a maximum behavioural complexity of significantly closer to five actions than the ADAPT agents. This is a property of the MMORL algorithm used in the RECALL agents. Each option learned by a MMORL agent represents the solution to exactly one task. No interleaving of tasks can occur using this model. In contrast the REUSE_INTEREST and REUSE_COMPETENCE agents achieve behavioural complexity that is significantly higher than that required to perform the most complex task in the environment. This is because the MHRL approach they use allows hierarchical behavioural policies that comprise multiple options for performing different tasks.

Figure 7.8 shows the rate at which behavioural variety is actually acquired by three of the agents motivated to achieve interesting events. ADAPT_INTEREST agents initially learn behaviours very quickly. In addition, they learn significantly more behaviours than RECALL_INTEREST and REUSE_INTEREST agents in the same time period. RECALL_INTEREST and REUSE_INTEREST agents learn more slowly and learn fewer behavioural cycles overall.

The behavioural variety attained by all the agents is significantly lower than the number of potential learning tasks (fifty-three) in the environment. This is important as it shows that the agents have focused their attention on a subset of tasks in their environment. In complex environments it is frequently infeasible for agents to learn every task. In certain such environments, characters that attempt to learn every task are likely to be at a disadvantage because there are simply too many tasks to learn.

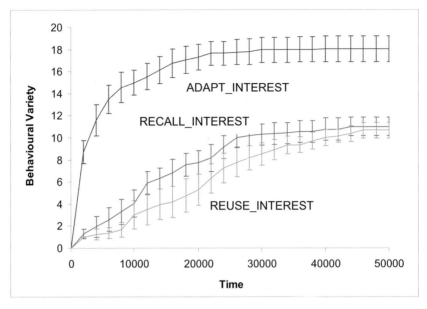

Fig. 7.8 Cumulative behavioural variety by three of the agents motivated to achieve interesting events.

7.3 Summary

This chapter compared six different MRL agent models for controlling NPCs, using different motivation and learning models. These models were used to control NPCs in a small-scale, isolated village scenario, such as one that might be found as a scene in an adventure game or MMORPG. Perhaps the most exciting result of this demonstration was the ability of all the MRL agents to learn behavioural cycles that exhibit multitask learning using task-independent motivation signals computed based on an agent's experiences. Each agent developed a suite of behaviours to complete - different tasks, resulting in a cast of village characters including carpenters, blacksmiths and travellers. This means that it is possible for a single agent to be applied to multiple agents, which then develop into different characters based on their experiences in their environment.

A number of key differences were evident in the performance of the six types of MRL agent:

- The ADAPT agents both showed significantly higher variety and complexity of behaviour than the RECALL and REUSE agents.

- REUSE agents showed the highest behavioural variety and complexity of the agents that can recall or reuse learned behaviours.

These results suggest that there is a trade-off between the ability of NPCs using MRL to adapt quickly to changes in their environment and their ability to recall learned behaviours. The former type of NPC might be more valuable in highly dynamic game worlds, while the latter might be more useful when there is a high chance that past events will be repeated. The ADAPT agents also developed the highest behavioural complexity. This implies NPCs capable of longer, more interesting behavioural cycles that interleave solutions to multiple tasks.

The next chapter considers larger-scale settings in which characters have greater freedom to move to more locations and perform more complex tasks.

7.4 References

[1]   Linden, Second Life, www.secondlife.com (Accessed January, 2007).

[2]   K. Merrick and M.L. Maher, Motivated reinforcement learning for non-player characters in persistent computer game worlds, International Conference on Advances in Computer Entertainment Technology, 2006, CA, USA (electronic proceedings).

Chapter 8
Curious Characters for Games in Complex, Dynamic Environments

Complex, dynamic environments pose a number of challenges for learning agents. A complex environment has many objects, events, and potential tasks to be learned which results in a very large search space. The size of the search space increases exponentially since a potential state can be any combination of all possible states for any object. This exponential increase can have a dramatic effect on the ability of the learning agent to achieve a specific task.

Dynamic environments are those in which the objects in the environment can change over time: some disappearing from the environment and others appearing after the learning agent has started. This poses a challenge for a learning agent if the agent is maintaining a memory of tasks learned and the action that it remembers is on an object that no longer exists. A second challenge in dynamic environments is the introduction of new objects into the state space representation and altering the clustering and similarity comparisons from the past experience.

In this chapter we show how motivated reinforcement learning agents respond differently in selectively complex and dynamic environments. We once again study the six different kinds of motivated reinforcement learning agents for non-player characters introduced in Chap. 7. The studies in Chap. 7 investigated the emergent behaviour of these agents in small-scale, isolated game scenarios. This chapter builds on Chap. 7 by exploring the six types of agents in more complex and dynamic MMORPG scenarios. Three different types of game locations are considered in the following sections: locations where characters have many tasks to learn, locations where the tasks are complex, and locations where the tasks can change while characters are learning and interacting with the game environment.

K.E. Merrick, M.L. Maher, *Motivated Reinforcement Learning*, DOI 10.1007/978-3-540-89187-1_8,
© Springer-Verlag Berlin Heidelberg 2009

8.1 Designing Characters That Can Multitask

The previous chapter introduced a simulated game environment modelled as two Markov decision processes (MDPs), P_1 and P_2. P_1 contained the objects required to mine iron-ore and forge weapons and P_2 contained the objects required to cut timber and craft furniture. This section extends that scenario with four additional MDPs, P_3, P_4, P_5 and P_6 for tasks in the environment shown in Fig. 8.1. New tasks include farming, fishing, pottery and wine-making.

P_3 has the same structure as P_1 but additional tasks for collecting grain, milling flour and making bread as shown in Fig. 8.2. P_4 has additional tasks for collecting clay, making pottery and firing pottery as shown in Fig. 8.3. P_5, described by the context-free grammar (CFG) in Fig. 8.4, includes additional tasks for fishing, preparing a fish fillet and cooking fish. Finally P_6 includes tasks for picking grapes, pressing the grapes and making wine, as shown in Fig. 8.5. The aim of this section is to investigate the behaviour of the different types of motivated reinforcement learning (MRL) agents in game scenarios with more potential learning tasks.

Fig. 8.1 A visualisation in *Second Life* of part of the simulated game scenario with multiple tasks.

K.E. Merrick, M.L. Maher

Motivated Reinforcement Learning

Erratum

Due to a technical error, Fig. 8.1 on page 152 was not printed correctly.
Please find the correct figure below:

```
<P₃Sensations>          →   <P₃location><P₃inventory><P₃visibleObjects>
<P₃location>            →   <grain field> | <flour mill>
<grain field>          →   5
<flour mill>           →   6
<P₃inventory>           →   <P₃objects>
<P₃visibleObjects>      →   <P₃objects>
<P₃objects>             →   <P₃object><P₃objects> | ε
<P₃object>              →   <scythe> | <mill> | <oven> | <wheat> |
                            <flour> | <bread>
<scythe>               →   1
<mill>                 →   1
<oven>                 →   1
<wheat>                →   1
<flour>                →   1
<bread>                →   1
- - - - - - - - - - - - - - - - - - - - - - - - - - - - - - - - - - - - - - - -
<P₃Actions>             →   pick-up <P₃object> | move <direction> |
                            use <P₃object>
<direction>            →   north | south | east | west
<P₃object>              →   scythe | mill | oven | wheat | flour |
                            bread
```

Fig. 8.2 State and action spaces for the additional MDP P_3 for a farm.

```
<P₄Sensations>          →   <P₄location><P₄inventory><P₄visibleObjects>
<P₄location>            →   <clay pit> | <potter>
<clay pit>             →   7
<potter>               →   8
<P₄inventory>           →   <P₄objects>
<P₄visibleObjects>      →   <P₄objects>
<P₄objects>             →   <P₄object><P₄objects> | ε
<P₄object>              →   <spade> | <pottery wheel> | <kiln> |
                            <clay> | <pottery> | <fired pottery>
<spade>                →   1
<pottery wheel>        →   1
<kiln>                 →   1
<clay>                 →   1
<pottery>              →   1
<fired pottery>        →   1
- - - - - - - - - - - - - - - - - - - - - - - - - - - - - - - - - - - - - - - -
<P₄Actions>             →   pick-up <P₄object> | move <direction> |
                            use <P₄object>
<direction>            →   north | south | east | west
<P₄object>              →   spade | pottery wheel | kiln | clay |
                            pottery
```

Fig. 8.3 State and action spaces for the additional MDP P_4 for a clay pit and potter.

```
<P₅Sensations>          →   <P₅location><P₅inventory><P₅visibleObjects>
<P₅location>            →   <river> | <small hut>
<river>                 →   9
<small hut>             →   10
<P₅inventory>           →   <P₅objects>
<P₅visibleObjects>      →   <P₅objects>
<P₅objects>             →   <P₅object><P₅objects> | ε
<P₅object>              →   <fishing line> | <knife> | <stove> |
                            <fish> | <fillet> | <cooked fish>
<fishing line>          →   1
<knife>                 →   1
<stove>                 →   1
<fish>                  →   1
<fillet>                →   1
<cooked fish>           →   1
----------------------------------------------------------------
<P₅Actions>             →   pick-up <P₅object> | move <direction> |
                            use <P₅object>
<direction>             →   north | south | east | west
<P₅object>              →   fishing line | knife | stove | fish |
                            fillet | cooked fish
```

Fig. 8.4 State and action spaces for the additional MDP P_5 for a river.

```
<P₆Sensations>          →   <P₆location><P₆inventory><P₆visibleObjects>
<P₆location>            →   <vineyard> | <winery>
<vineyard>              →   11
<winery>                →   12
<P₆inventory>           →   <P₆objects>
<P₆visibleObjects>      →   <P₆objects>
<P₆objects>             →   <P₆object><P₆objects> | ε
<P₆object>              →   <shears> | <press> | <cask> | <grapes> |
                            <pressed grapes> | <wine>
<shears>                →   1
<press>                 →   1
<cask>                  →   1
<grapes>                →   1
<pressed grapes>        →   1
<wine>                  →   1
----------------------------------------------------------------
<P₆Actions>             →   pick-up <P₆object> | move <direction> |
                            use <P₆object>
<direction>             →   north | south | east | west
<P₆object>              →   shears | press | cask | grapes | pressed
                            grapes | wine
```

Fig. 8.5 State and action spaces for the additional MDP P_6 for a vineyard and winery.

The addition of new MDPs representing the new game locations increases the size of the state and action sets from the scenarios in Chap. 7. The game scenario studied in this section has approximately 35,000 states that non-player characters (NPCs) may encounter and seventy actions they can use. The six types of agents introduced in Chap. 7, and also studied in this chapter, are:

- ADAPT_INTEREST: A MFRL agent motivated to achieve interesting events;

- ADAPT_COMPETENCE: A MFRL agent motivated by interest and competence;

- RECALL_INTEREST: A MMORL agent motivated to achieve interesting events;

- RECALL_COMPETENCE: A MMORL agent motivated by interest and competence;

- REUSE_INTEREST: A MHRL agent motivated to achieve interesting events;

- REUSE_COMPETENCE: A MHRL agent motivated by interest and competence.

We begin once again in Sect. 8.1.1 by studying the behaviour of the simplest agents using the ADAPT_INTEREST model. Two of these agents are studied over a period of 50,000 time steps in the environment described previously. This provides a baseline against which we can understand the behaviour of agents using the other models. In Sect. 8.1.2 we present a more general comparison of the behaviour of agents using all six models. Agents using each of the models were run twenty times, this time for 150,000 time-steps. The actions of each agent were logged and a statistical analysis of their behaviour made using the metrics from Chap. 4.

8.1.1   Case Studies of Individual Characters

Figure 8.6 shows the evolution of behavioural variety by two ADAPT_INTEREST agents over the first 50,000 time-steps of their life. Both agents initially increase their behavioural variety at a similar rate. However Agent 1 then begins to learn new behavioural cycles more slowly than Agent 2. Eventually Agent 1 stops learning new behavioural cycles, at approximately $t = 15,000$, and focuses its actions on those behavioural cycles already learned. In contrast, Agent 2 displays a faster rate of increase in behavioural variety and learns more behavioural cycles during its 50,000 time-step lifetime. The shape of the curve for Agent 2 suggests that, if this agent were run for longer, it would continue to learn more behavioural cycles, although at a relatively low rate.

The tasks learned by the two agents also differ. Some of the tasks learned by the two agents are shown by the labels in Fig. 8.6. In general, Agent 1 focuses on travelling tasks, particularly between the river, the potter and the small hut. Agent 2 focuses on travelling, picking wheat, making flour and bread and mining iron. This demonstrates that, even in this more complex environment, ADAPT_INTEREST agents are able to use the task-independent model of curiosity to learn structured behavioural cycles. In addition, agents using the same model can develop different characters based on their experiences.

Unlike the trends seen in Chap. 7, however, there is a significant difference between the emergent behaviour of ADAPT_INTEREST agents and agents using the other models. These differences are revealed in the next section.

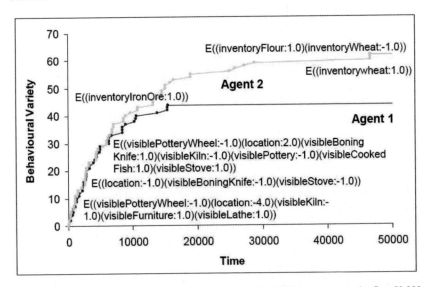

Fig. 8.6. Behavioural variety achieved by two ADAPT_INTEREST agents over the first 50,000 time-steps of their life.

8.1.2   *General Trends in Character Behaviour*

Figures 8.7 and 8.8 characterise the behaviour of the six different MRL agents in a game scenario with many learning tasks. ADAPT_INTEREST and ADAPT_COMPETENCE agents again show similar behavioural trends, with both showing behavioural variety of between 48 and 55 tasks and behavioural complexity of between six and eight. This is significantly higher than the other four models. While the increase in behavioural variety from that shown by the agents in Chap. 7 is significantly smaller than the increase in the number of potential learning tasks, this result still demonstrates how the behaviour of the agents has adapted to the more complex environment.

Figure 8.8 shows that ADAPT_INTEREST, ADAPT_COMPETENCE and RECALL_COMPETENCE agents have behavioural complexity significantly higher than that of the most complex task in the environment, which requires five actions to complete. In contrast agents using the other models limit their attention focus to the simple one and two action travelling tasks.

RECALL_INTEREST and both of the REUSE agents show the lowest behavioural variety and complexity in this environment. These agents learn only one task. An inspection of the log files for these agents reveals that this is the 'do nothing' task. While other interesting tasks are identified, high interest values are not maintained long enough for these tasks to be learned. This result is problematic because these agents with the ability to recall and reuse learned behaviours do not achieve multitask learning in this more complex environment. The decrease in behavioural variety and complexity when the number of potential learning tasks in the environment is increased is caused by the creation of larger numbers of options. When the number of options created is large, the branching factor of the MMORL and MHRL learning algorithm increases, placing demands on time and memory resources. Given enough time and memory, it is expected that all options created could be learned, but it would take significantly more time and memory resources to achieve similar behavioural variety to agents using MFRL.

However, RECALL_COMPETENCE agents do offer an approach to NPCs that can achieve both multitask learning and recall of learned behaviours. RECALL_COMPETENCE agents exhibit multitask learning with behavioural complexity that is at least as high as the most complex task in the environment. This performance difference is because agents that incorporate competence motivation are able to maintain high motivation for selected tasks until that task is learned. These results indicate that the trade-off between the need for recall and the need for a high rate of emergence of behavioural variety and complexity must be considered when selecting a MRL model for a particular application.

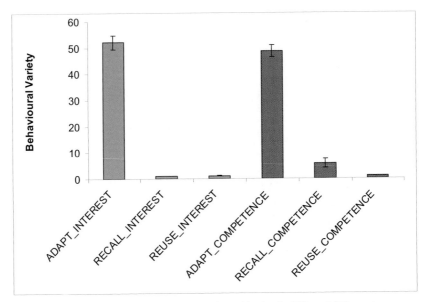

Fig. 8.7. Average behavioural variety achieved by the six different MRL agents.

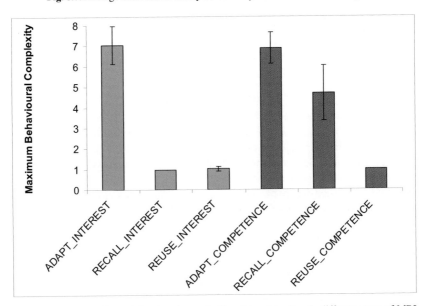

Fig. 8.8 Average maximum behavioural complexity achieved by the six different types of MRL agent.

8.2 Designing Characters for Complex Tasks

Where the previous section explored the behaviour of MRL techniques for characters in game scenarios with many potential learning tasks, this section explores their behaviour in a scenario with tasks requiring many actions to complete. The number of available tasks remains the same as the environment in Chap. 7 as no additional objects are added to the environment. Rather, existing tasks are made more complex by requiring existing actions to be applied in longer sequences to complete the task.

The most complex task in the small-scale game location in Chap. 7 required five actions to complete. The most complex task in the environment in this chapter requires thirteen actions to complete. This complexity is achieved by increasing the number of raw materials required to make a finished item from one to five. That is, an NPC must now chop five pieces of wood to make furniture and mine and smelt five units of iron to make weapons. The CFG describing the state and action spaces for this environment is shown in Fig. 8.9. This environment has approximately 1000 states and twenty-four actions.

The same six types of agents are studied as in the previous section. We again begin by studying the emergent behaviour of the simple ADAPT_INTEREST agents in Sect. 8.2.1, then compare this behaviour to that of the other five models in Sect. 8.2.2. Each of these agents was run twenty times for 150,000 time-steps in this environment.

8.2.1   Case Studies of Individual Characters

Figure 8.10 shows behavioural cycles learned by three different ADAPT_INTEREST agents. The first cycle comprises eleven actions to collect wood and make furniture. The second cycle comprises twenty-nine actions to move, gather raw materials and use the lathe, smelt and forge to make furniture and weapons. These examples illustrate how the behaviour of MRL agents can adapt to environments with more complex tasks. These behavioural cycles also show how ADAPT_INTEREST agents can either learn behavioural cycles for individual tasks or interleave the actions for multiple tasks within a complex behavioural cycle.

The third cycle comprises fifty-eight actions for travelling between different locations, gathering raw materials and using the various tools. While this behavioural cycle does not represent an optimal policy for weapons making or furniture making, it does represent optimal accumulation of curiosity reward. This example shows that MRL agents can evolve complex, repeated behaviour cycles with interesting variations unique to individual characters.

```
S                       →    <sensations>
<sensations>            →    <P₁Sensations><P₂Sensations>
<P₁Sensations>          →    <P₁location><P₁inventory><P₁visibleObjects>
<P₁location>            →    <mine> | <smithy>
<mine>                  →    1
<smithy>                →    2
<P₁inventory>           →    <P₁objects>
<P₁visibleObjects>      →    <P₁objects>
<P₁objects>             →    <P₁object><P₁objects> | ε
<P₁object>              →    <pick> | <forge> | <smelt> | <iron-ore> |
                             <iron> | <weapons>
<P₂Sensations>          →    <P₂location><P₂inventory><P₂visibleObjects>
<P₂location>            →    <forest> | <carpenter-shop>
<forest>                →    3
<carpenter-shop>        →    4
<P₂inventory>           →    <P₂objects>
<P₂visibleObjects>      →    <P₂objects>
<P₂objects>             →    <P₂object><P₂objects> | ε
<P₂object>              →    <axe> | <lathe> | <timber> | <furniture>
<pick>                  →    1
<forge>                 →    1
<smelt>                 →    1
<iron-ore>              →    1 | 2 | 3 | 4 | 5
<iron>                  →    1 | 2 | 3 | 4 | 5
<weapons>               →    1
<axe>                   →    1
<lathe>                 →    1
<timber>                →    1 | 2 | 3 | 4 | 5
<furniture>             →    1
- - - - - - - - - - - - - - - - - - - - - - - - - - - - - - - - - - - - - -
A                       →    <actions>
<actions>               →    <P₁Actions><P₂Actions>
<P₁Actions>             →    pick-up <P₁object> | move <direction> |
                             use <P₁object>
<P₂Actions>             →    pick-up <P₂object> | move <direction> |
                             use <P₂object>
<direction>             →    north | south | east | west
<P₁object>              →    pick | forge | smelt | iron | iron-ore |
                             weapons
<P₂object>              →    axe | lathe | timber | furniture
```

Fig. 8.9 State and action spaces of an environment with complex tasks.

(a) Move north → Use axe → Use axe → Use axe → Use axe → Use axe
▲ → Move west → Move south → Move east → Use lathe ⌐

(b) Move south → Use smelt → Use smelt → Use smelt → Move east→
Move north → Use axe → Use axe → Use axe → Move west → Use
▲ pick → Use pick → Use pick → Move south → Use smelt → Move
north → Use pick → Move east → Move south → Use lathe → Move
north → Use axe → Use axe → Move south → Move west → Use
forge → Use smelt → Move north → Use pick ⌐

(c) Use lathe → Move north → Move west → Move south → Use smelt →
Use smelt→ Use smelt → Move east → Move west → Use smelt →
▲ Move north → Use pick → Move south → Use smelt → Move north
→ Move south → Move north → Move east → Use axe → Move
south → Move west → Use forge → Use smelt → Move north →
Use pick → Move east → Use axe → Move south → Move west →
Use smelt → Move north → Use pick → Use pick → Move east →
Use axe → Move south → Move west → Use smelt → Move north
→ Use pick → Use pick → Move south → Use smelt → Move north
→ Move east → Use axe → Use axe → Move west → Use pick →
Use pick → Move south → Use smelt → Move north → Use pick →
Use pick → Move south → Use forge → Move east ⌐

Fig. 8.10 Examples of behaviour cycle evolved by three different ADAPT_INTEREST agents.

8.2.2 General Trends in Character Behaviour

Figures 8.11 and 8.12 characterise the behaviour of NPCs using the different agent models in an environment with more complex tasks. Fig. 8.12 shows that ADAPT and RECALL agents all achieve behavioural complexity that is at least as high as the number of actions (thirteen) required to achieve the most complex task. In addition, both of the ADAPT agents display behavioural complexity that is significantly higher than thirteen actions. This shows that agents using these models can interleave the solutions to multiple tasks as behavioural cycles. In contrast, RECALL agents using MMORL learn options for individual tasks so their emergent behavioural complexity is much closer to that of the tasks present in the environment.

The REUSE agents using MHRL show significantly lower behavioural variety and maximum behavioural complexity than the other four agent models. The reason for this is that MHRL agents can reuse options as abstract

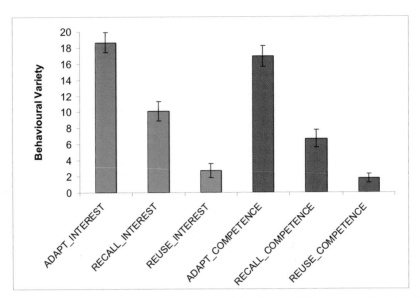

Fig. 8.11. Maximum behavioural variety achieved by the six different types of motivated reinforcement learning agents.

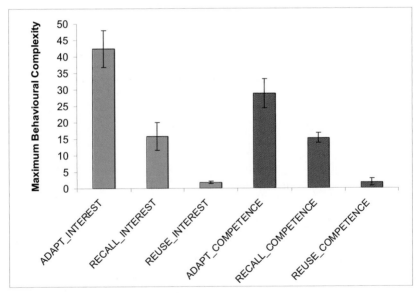

Fig. 8.12 Average maximum behavioural complexity achieved by the six different types of motivated reinforcement learning agents.

actions while learning new options. This increases the branching factor of learning for later options as there are more abstract actions to choose from. Previous work with hierarchical reinforcement learning (HRL) has shown that, when abstract actions are chosen carefully, the speed of learning can be increased. However, if too many abstract actions are used, the speed of learning is decreased. In the MHRL model, a reflex disables options that are not learned within a certain time period to prevent agents attempting to learn tasks that are no longer relevant.

8.3 Games That Change While Characters Are Learning

Chapter 7 introduced a simulated game environment modelled as two MDPs, P_1 and P_2. P_1 contained the objects required to mine iron-ore and forge weapons and P_2 contained the objects required to cut timber and craft furniture. This section explores the behaviour of MRL agents when their environment can change while learning is in progress, such that existing tasks become impossible to achieve and new tasks emerging. This is modelled by changing the environment while learning is in progress so that it is no longer modelled by P_1 and P_2 but by two new MDPs, P_3 and P_4.

Initially, the simulated game environment is identical to the one described in Chap. 7. After 50,000 time-steps, the environment is changed such that the initial MDPs, P_1 and P_2, are replaced by two new MDPs, P_3 and P_4. P_1 and P_2 describe states and actions that allowed activities such as travelling, mining iron-ore, forging weapons, cutting timber and crafting furniture. At $t = 50,000$, monsters spawn as shown in Fig. 8.13. The monsters damage the forge and the lathe so that the actions for using the forge or lathe no longer produce weapons or furniture. Instead, however, if the pick or axe are used on a monster, the monster will die. Dead monsters disappear and new monsters spawn when the agent moves away from the dead monster's location. The state and action sets for P_3 and P_4 are shown in Fig 8.14.

The size of the state space decreases dramatically from fifty-two to eight states due to the destruction of the forge and lathe, although the exact set of states in the new state space depends on the state at $t = 50,000$ when the environment changes. The size of the action space increases slightly by two actions with the addition of the monster. As a result, the number of tasks in the environment after the change also decreases to twelve tasks including four from the original MDPs for travelling between the forest and the mine and between the smithy and the carpenter's shop. MRL agents that exhibit adaptable behaviour in this environment should, after the change, display an increase in behavioural variety that is significantly greater than four tasks.

The results in this section compare the behaviour of the six different MRL agents. Each of these agents was run twenty times for 100,000 time-steps, with the environment changing at $t = 50{,}000$ time-steps. Section 8.3.1 studies the emergent behaviour of one ADAPT_INTEREST agent over this period. Section 8.3.2 compares these agents to those using the other five models.

8.3.1   Case Studies of Individual Characters

Chapter 7 compared the average focus of attention of two agents over 50,000 time-steps. Figure 7.5 showed how different agents are motivated to focus their learning on different tasks in response to their different experiences in their environment. In contrast, Fig. 8.15 traces the change in attention focus exhibited by one agent motivated by interest and competence in response to its experiences in a changing environment. The lifetime of this agent is broken into four phases: $t = 0{-}25{,}000$, $t = 25{,}001{-}50{,}000$, $t = 50{,}001{-}75{,}000$ and $t = 75{,}001{-}100{,}000$ and progressive change in attention focus charted between these phases. Figure 8.15 shows that, at the end of the first phase, the primary focus of attention is on tasks represented by events E_1–E_{10}. These are travelling tasks, timber cutting and furniture making. By the end of the second phase, the agent's focus of attention has shifted slightly, away from tasks E_4, E_6, E_9 and E_{10}, and towards tasks E_{13}–E_{17}. In the third phase, during which the environment changes, another shift in attention focus occurs. By the end of the third phase the agent's attention is focused primarily on tasks E_{21}–E_{30}. Only four tasks, E_3, E_5, E_7 and E_8, remain from the initial phase. This focus of attention remains stable throughout the fourth phase.

Fig. 8.13 A visualisation in *Second Life* of the simulated game scenario after a monster has appeared. Image from [1].

```
S                           →   <sensations>
<sensations>                →   <P₄Sensations><P₅Sensations>
<P₄Sensations>              →   <P₄location><P₄inventory><P₄visibleObjects>
<P₄location>                →   <mine> | <smithy>
<mine>                      →   1
<smithy>                    →   2
<P₄inventory>               →   <P₄objects>
<P₄visibleObjects>          →   <P₄objects>
<P₄objects>                 →   <P₄object><P₄objects> | ε
<P₄object>                  →   <pick> | <forge> | <smelt> | <iron-ore> |
                                <iron> | <weapons> | <monster> |
                                <dead monster>
<P₅Sensations>              →   <P₅location><P₅inventory><P₅visibleObjects>
<P₅location>                →   <forest> | <carpenter-shop>
<forest>                    →   3
<carpenter-shop>            →   4
<P₅inventory>               →   <P₅objects>
<P₅visibleObjects>          →   <P₅objects>
<P₅objects>                 →   <P₅object><P₅objects> | ε
<P₅object>                  →   <axe> | <lathe> | <timber> | <furniture> |
                                <monster> | <dead monster>
<pick>                      →   1
<forge>                     →   1
<smelt>                     →   1
<iron-ore>                  →   1
<iron>                      →   1
<weapons>                   →   1
<axe>                       →   1
<lathe>                     →   1
<timber>                    →   1
<furniture>                 →   1
<monster>                   →   1
<dead monster>              →   1
- - - - - - - - - - - - - - - - - - - - - - - - - - - - - - - - - - - - - -
A                           →   <actions>
<actions>                   →   <P₄Actions><P₅Actions>
<P₄Actions>                 →   pick-up <P₄object> | move <direction> | use
                                <P₄object>
<P₅Actions>                 →   pick-up <P₅object> | move <direction> | use
                                <P₅object>
<direction>                 →   north | south | east | west
<P₄object>                  →   pick | forge | smelt | iron | iron-ore |
                                weapons | monster | dead monster
<P₅object>                  →   axe | lathe | timber | furniture | monster
                                | dead monster
```

Fig. 8.14 State and action spaces of the environment in Experiment 4 after $t = 50,000$.

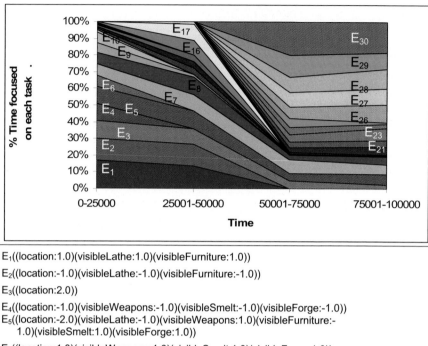

E_1((location:1.0)(visibleLathe:1.0)(visibleFurniture:1.0))

E_2((location:-1.0)(visibleLathe:-1.0)(visibleFurniture:-1.0))

E_3((location:2.0))

E_4((location:-1.0)(visibleWeapons:-1.0)(visibleSmelt:-1.0)(visibleForge:-1.0))
E_5((location:-2.0)(visibleLathe:-1.0)(visibleWeapons:1.0)(visibleFurniture:-1.0)(visibleSmelt:1.0)(visibleForge:1.0))

E_6((location:1.0)(visibleWeapons:1.0)(visibleSmelt:1.0)(visibleForge:1.0))

E_7((location:-2.0))
E_8((location:2.0)(visibleLathe:1.0)(visibleWeapons:-1.0)(visibleFurniture:1.0)(visibleSmelt:-1.0)(visibleForge:-1.0))

E_9((inventoryLog:1.0))

E_{10}((inventoryLog:-1.0))

E_{16}((location:1.0)(visibleAxe:1.0)(visibleLathe:1.0))

E_{17}((location:-1.0)(visibleAxe:-1.0)(visibleLathe:-1.0))
E_{21}((visibleMonster:-1.0)(location:-1.0)(visibleDeadMonster:-1.0)(visibleWeapons:-1.0)(visibleSmelt:-1.0)(visibleForge:-1.0))
E_{23}((visibleMonster:1.0)(location:-2.0)(visibleLathe:-1.0)(visibleWeapons:1.0)(visibleFurniture:-1.0)(visibleSmelt:1.0)(visibleForge:1.0))
E_{26}((visibleMonster:-1.0)(location:-1.0)(visibleLathe:-1.0)(visibleDeadMonster:-1.0)(visibleFurniture:-1.0))

E_{27}((visibleMonster:1.0)(location:1.0)(visibleLathe:1.0)(visibleFurniture:1.0))
E_{28}((visibleMonster:1.0)(location:2.0)(visibleLathe:1.0)(visibleWeapons:-1.0)(visibleFurniture:1.0)(visibleSmelt:-1.0)(visibleForge:-1.0))

E_{29}((visibleMonster:1.0)(location:1.0)(visibleWeapons:1.0)(visibleSmelt:1.0)(visibleForge:1.0))

E_{30}((visibleMonster:-1.0)(visibleDeadMonster:1.0))

Fig. 8.15 Change in attention focus over time exhibited by a single agent motivated by interest and competence in a dynamic environment.

8.3.2   General Trends in Character Behaviour

Figure 8.16 illustrates the effect of changes in the environment on the behavioural cycles learned by ADAPT agents using different motivation functions. During the period $t = 20,000$ to $t = 50,000$ the gradient of the behavioural variety curves does not alter for any of the agent types. In the case of the agents motivated to achieve interesting events or motivated by interest and competency, the gradients of these curves is close to zero. This suggests that no new behaviours are being learned in that time period. After $t = 50,000$ when the environment changes with the appearance of monsters, the cumulative behavioural variety of these agents increases significantly by between seven and twelve behaviours. This indicates that learning of new behavioural cycles is occurring for tasks such as running towards a monster, killing a monster or running away from a monster.

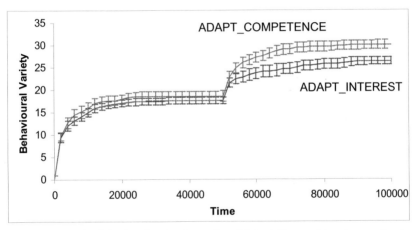

Fig. 8.16 Cumulative behavioural variety by motivated flat reinforcement learning agents using different motivation functions.

After the monsters appear at $t = 50,000$, the increase in behavioural variety by ADAPT_COMPETENCE agents is significantly higher than that of the ADAPT_INTEREST agents. The motivation to develop new competencies allows agents to focus attention on and learn behavioural cycles for new tasks more quickly than interest motivation alone. This suggests that in simple, dynamic environments, ADAPT_COMPETENCE are more adaptable than those motivated by interest alone. This is due to their preference for pursuing tasks of low competency before tasks of low interest.

Figure 8.17 shows that RECALL agents also show a significant increase in behavioural variety after $t = 50,000$ of between six and ten behaviours. However, this is smaller than the increase shown by ADAPT agents. RECALL_COMPETENCE agents show slightly higher adaptability than

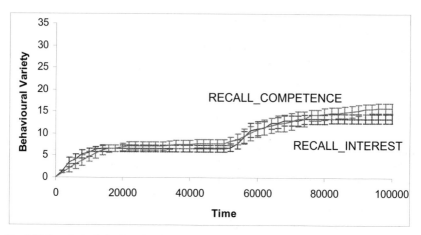

Fig. 8.17 Cumulative behavioural variety by motivated, multioption reinforcement learning agents using different motivation functions.

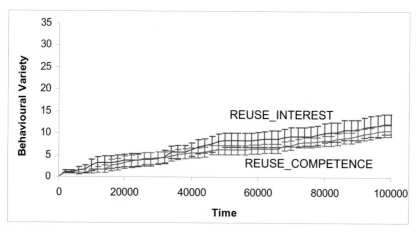

Fig. 8.18 Cumulative behavioural variety by motivated hierarchical reinforcement learning agents using different motivation functions.

RECALL_INEREST agents. Figure 8.18 shows that REUSE agents also achieve a significant increase in behavioural variety after $t = 50,000$ of between three and seven behaviours. In this case, however, there is little difference between the performance of different motivation functions.

8.4 Summary

The studies in this chapter reveal a number of different properties of the behaviour of NPCs using the six MRL models in complex and dynamic environments. Two broad types of responses were exhibited by MRL agents in the different environments. In some cases, behavioural variety and complexity were either the same or higher than that seen by the same agents in Chap. 7. The second type of response was a decrease in either behavioural variety or complexity. This type of response is generally undesirable as the limiting case is agents characterised by the ability to do nothing at all in complex environments.

In each of the different game scenarios, ADAPT agents without recall showed greater changes in their behaviour than the RECALL and REUSE agents. In the multitasking environment, for example, the ADAPT agents develop complex behavioural cycles of more than fifty actions, compared to around ten actions in the simpler environment in Chap. 7. Similarly, in the dynamic environment the ADAPT_COMPETENCE agents show the largest change in behavioural variety in response to the monsters.

Of the approaches with recall, the RECALL_COMPETENCE agents appear the most adaptable. These agents displayed significantly higher behavioural variety and complexity than the REUSE agents in the same environments.

The studies in this chapter highlight the tradeoffs between the different MRL models. The ADAPT agents are clearly highly adaptable, but cannot recall or reuse learned behaviours. These models are thus most likely to be useful for NPCs in highly dynamic environments that are undergoing constant evolution. The RECALL and REUSE agents can remember learned behaviours, but do not adapt as quickly to change. These models, in their current form, are most appropriate for characters in simple, isolated game scenarios where the recall mechanism does not impact so highly on learning.

In the next chapter we study the most adaptive model seen so far, ADAPT_COMPETENCE, for the control of NPCs in a live virtual world.

8.5 References

[1] K. Merrick, Modelling motivation for adaptive non-player characters in dynamic computer game worlds. ACM Computers in Entertainment 5(4), 2007.

Chapter 9
Curious Characters for Games in *Second Life*

Recently, a new generation of multiuser virtual worlds has emerged in which users are provided with open-ended modelling tools with which they can create and modify world content. The result is evolving virtual spaces for commerce, education, entertainment and social interaction. In general, these virtual worlds are not games and have no concept of winning. However the open-ended modelling capacity is nonetheless compelling. The rising popularity of open-ended virtual worlds such as *Second Life* [1] and *There* [2] suggests that there may also be potential for a new generation of computer games situated in open-ended environments. A key issue with the development of such games, however, is the design of non-player characters that can respond autonomously to unpredictable, open-ended changes to their environment.

This chapter considers the impact of open-ended modelling on character development in simulation games and introduces motivated reinforcement learning as a means of creating non-player characters that can respond to unpredictable, evolving worlds.

9.1 Motivated Reinforcement Learning in Open-Ended Simulation Games

The idea of an open-ended simulation game extends the existing simulation game genre with open-ended modelling tools. We designed an open-ended simulation game called *Aussie Outback Challenge* in the *Second Life* [1] virtual world as an experimental application for motivated reinforcement learning (MRL) agents. The following sections describe the design of this game, the application of MRL agents to character control and the behaviour of the resulting characters during game sequences.

K.E. Merrick, M.L. Maher, *Motivated Reinforcement Learning*, DOI 10.1007/978-3-540-89187-1_9,
© Springer-Verlag Berlin Heidelberg 2009

9.1.1   Game Design

Aussie Outback Challenge is an open-ended, persistent simulation game set in the *Second Life* virtual environment [3]. The game is set on a sheep farm with six 'uncommonly intelligent sheep'. The aim of the game is to build challenges that will attract the interest of as many sheep as possible. As a persistent simulation game, the game does not 'end'. Rather the winner at any particular time is the player whose challenge is currently attracting the attention of the most sheep.

The game play area is 1,968 square metres of virtual land situated on a main road as shown in Fig. 9.1(a). In the opening sequence of the game, each new player is directed by a sign from the main road to a barn, shown in Fig. 9.1(b) where they receive instructions. The instructions, shown in Fig. 9.1(c), direct players to the sheep food machine shown in Fig. 9.1(d) which is an example of a successful game play sequence. Players can copy the food machine object and scripts to use in their own game play. They are then on their own to start the game. Players can use any of the *Second Life* modelling tools shown in Fig. 9.2 or the scripting tools shown in Fig. 9.1(e) to design challenges and attempt to attract the attention of one or more sheep.

9.1.2   Character Design

The non-player characters (NPCs) in *Aussie Outback Challenge* are the six 'uncommonly intelligent sheep'. The sheep need to be able to show interest in, adapt to and learn about any challenge built for them. However the exact nature of these challenges is not known by game designers prior to the game beginning. Thus, MRL approaches are an appropriate solution for character control where traditional reflex and learning agent approaches are not.

The key requirement for the sheep characters is that they be able to adapt rapidly to changes in their environment. The studies in the previous chapters showed that ADAPT_COMPETENCE agents adapt the most rapidly and develop the highest behavioural variety in dynamic environments. As these are advantageous abilities for this game, this combination is selected for the control of the sheep characters.

NPCs can be created in *Second Life* by connecting an agent program written in a programming language such as *Java* to a 3D model of the character, in this case a sheep, using the framework shown in Fig. 9.3. The *Java* agent program consists of sensor stubs, agent reasoning processes and effector stubs. The *Java* sensor and effector stubs act as clients that connect via XML-RPC to corresponding sensor and effector stubs written in the *Linden Scripting Langauge* (LSL) and residing on a *Second Life* server. LSL sensor

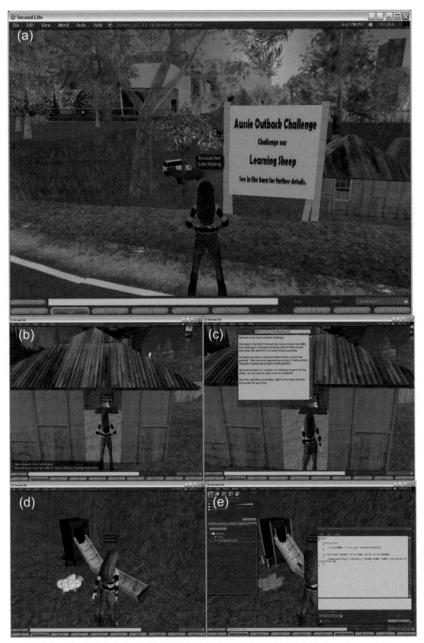

Fig. 9.1 Opening sequences of *Aussie Outback Challenge*, an open-ended, persistent simulation game set in the *Second Life* virtual world. **(a)** Players view the game from the road. **(b)** Players enter the shed and **(c)** receive instructions. **(d)** Player views an example of game play. **(e)** Player begins to design their own challenges for the sheep.

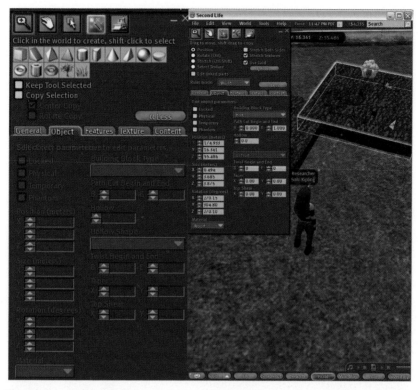

Fig. 9.2 Open-ended modelling tools in *Second Life*. Avatars can create primitive shapes then modify their dimensions, position, twist, hollow, taper, shear, and so on.

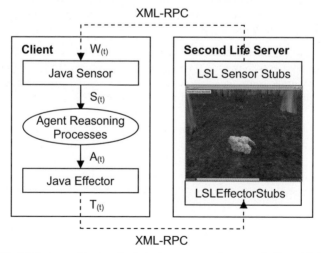

Fig. 9.3 System architecture for designing agents as characters for *Second Life*.

and effector stubs are associated with each sheep allowing them to sense, reason about and affect their environment.

In *Aussie Outback Challenge*, the sheep are ADAPT_COMPETENCE agents with sensors enabling them to monitor objects, avatars and their location in the world and effectors allowing them to move to or use objects and avatars:

- Object sensor: monitors the environment and returns data describing objects within a six metre radius of the sheep. Data includes the name and quantity of the object. Sheep cannot sense other sheep.[3]

- Avatar sensor: monitors the environment and returns data describing avatars within a six metre radius of the sheep. Data includes the name of the avatar.

- Location sensor: monitors the environment and returns a sheep's location as the id of closest object within a three-metre radius or 'nowhere' otherwise.

- Move to object effector: moves this sheep to the given object within a six-metre radius by applying a constant force over one second.

- Jump to object effector: moves this sheep to the given object with a four-to-six metre radius by applying an upwards impulse and a directional force over one second.

- Use object effector: triggers a behaviour to be executed by the given object. Object behaviours may include any action scripted by a player – such as a change in the object or the creation of new objects and so on.

While the set of sensors and effectors is fixed, the sensations they may return and the effects they may have on the environment are not. There is, for example, no predefined set of objects or avatars that may be sensed. Any player avatar may build and uniquely name any object to attempt to attract the attention of a sheep. Likewise, there is no predefined set of behavioural responses a 'usable' object may have to a sheep's attempt to use it. The 'use object effector' in particular adds complexity to an otherwise simple game by allowing players to express their creativity by designing objects that respond in novel, and hopefully interesting, ways to the sheep's attempts to use them. This can be seen in the game play sequences described in the next section.

---

[3] When sheep can sense each other, the emergent learned behaviour resembles flocking. While an interesting phenomenon, this flocking makes it more difficult for players to attract the attention of sheep. However, it could perhaps be used as an 'advanced' game setting.

9.2 Evaluating Character Behaviour in Response to Game Play Sequences

Initially, the game begins with six identical sheep. The sheep are located in a paddock as shown in Fig. 9.4. Initially, objects in the paddock included the food machine, a truck, a water trough and various rocks, trees and grasses. Over time, players used the *Second Life* modelling and scripting tools to remove existing objects and build new objects with which the sheep could interact. This section describes the behaviour of different sheep in response to some of the changes in their environment. The CFG representation of the environment constructed by sheep in response to their environment and the behavioural cycles they learn are also described.

Prior to the appearance of the player avatars, one of the sheep could sense a tuft of eelgrass:

$$S_{(1)} = (\texttt{<Eelgrass:3><location:Eelgrass>})$$

and thus had an action set:

$$\mathbf{A}_{(1)} = \{\texttt{move to(Eelgrass)}, \texttt{use(Eelgrass)}\}$$

Because the available sensations and the action set were limited to sensations and actions concerning the eelgrass, the sheep could only be motivated to learn about the eelgrass. It experimented with actions such as `move to(Eelgrass)` and `use(Eelgrass)`; however these actions produced no events as the sheep was already at the eelgrass and the eelgrass does not trigger a scripted response when used. The appearance of new objects or avatars is thus likely to trigger the emergence of new behaviours by this sheep.

In the one game play sequence a player, represented by an avatar called Sahi Kipling, moves the avatar close to the sheep. The state sensed by the sheep changes to:

$$S_{(2)} = ((\texttt{<Eelgrass:3><location:Eelgrass><Sahi Kipling:1>})$$

and the action set to:

$$\mathbf{A}_{(2)} = \{\texttt{move to(Eelgrass)}, \texttt{use(Eelgrass)}, \texttt{move to(Sahi Kipling)}, \texttt{jump to(Sahi Kipling)}\}$$

The sensed states and action sets change in response to the changing environment, and represent the objects and avatars currently sensed by a sheep. The sheep are now able to experiment with new actions and a motivation signal is computed based on the interest and competence the sheep computes for events resulting from each action attempted. The sheep experiments with the `move to(Sahi Kipling)` and `jump to(Sahi Kipling)` actions. These actions produce an event indicating that the sheep has changed its location:

$$E_{(2)} = (location(1))$$

The player progressively moves their avatar away from the sheep so the sheep continues to have a `move to(Sahi Kipling)` action in its action set that triggers a location change event when performed. Interest in this event increases according to the Wundt curve, eventually reinforcing the `move to(Sahi Kipling)` action so that an emergent 'following' behaviour is learned. This allows the player to draw the sheep away from the grass towards another part of the world as shown in Fig. 9.5(a). Figure 9.5(b) shows the behavioural cycle learned by the sheep in response to the player avatar.

The emergent following behaviour is not, however, limited to the move action. Over time, sheep also experiment with the jump action and learn 'following' behaviours using this action. This behavioural cycle is shown in Fig. 9.5(c). The emergence of either of the two following behaviours depends on the actions with which a sheep experiments. Sheep that experiment differently have different experiences and may thus develop one or both of the following behaviours.

Fig. 9.4 In *Aussie Outback Challenge*, six uncommonly intelligent sheep are located in a paddock in *Second Life*.

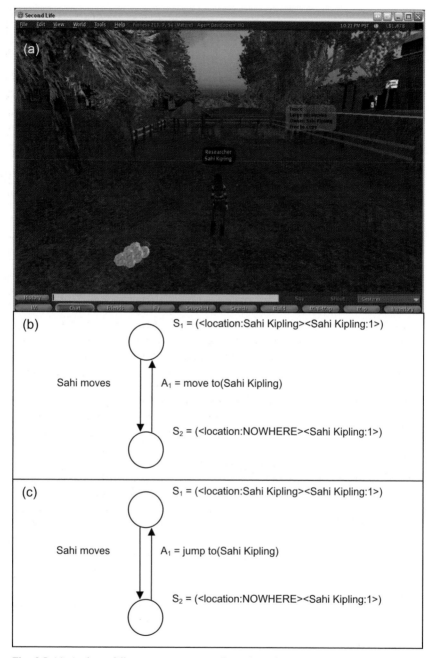

Fig. 9.5 (a) A sheep follows an avatar away from the eelgrass. **(b)** Finite state automaton representation of the learned 'following' behavioural cycle. **(c)** Representation of a different learned 'following' behavioural cycle.

In another game play sequence, shown in Fig. 9.6(a), a sheep has followed a player to the food machine. The food machine is scripted so that, should the sheep choose to use it, food will appear and slide down the shoot. The food, when used (eaten), will disappear. The state sensed by the sheep near the food machine in Fig. 9.6(a) is:

$$S_{(1)} = (<\text{Food machine:1}><\text{Food:2}><\text{location:Food machine}>)$$

and its action set is:

$$\mathbf{A}_{(1)} = \{\text{move to(Food), jump to(Food), use(Food), move to (Food Machine), use(Food)}\}$$

This example shows how the context free grammar (CFG) representation allows the sheep to adapt to its new setting. Only the sensations and actions relevant to its current situation are included in the sensed state and action set. Unlike fixed-length representations that would be required to maintain a representation of Sahi Kipling and the eelgrass even after they are no long relevant, the CFG represents only the data currently sensed by the learning agent. In the game scenario, this allows a sheep to experiment with just the actions relevant to its current situation, and to adapt its representation when its current situation changes.

As the sheep experiments with each available action, a motivation value is computed indicating the interest and competence level of the event caused by each action. These motivation values again reinforce certain actions, focus learning and stimulating the emergence of new behaviours.

Because motivation is based on experience and the experience of each sheep is different, different behavioural responses to the same situation are possible. This was observed with the food machine, for example. Some sheep moved between the red button and the food shoot, alternately using the button and a food ball. This behavioural cycle is shown in Fig. 9.6(b). Other sheep would use the button two or three times then use (eat) two or three food balls at once as shown in Fig. 9.6(c). Yet another sheep wedged itself on the shoot so that it could reach and use the food machine button while allowing the food to effectively roll into its mouth. It could use the food machine and food without needing to move at all as shown in Fig. 9.6(d).

The sheep interact with players and their environment in real time as the players modify their environment. Figure 9.7(a) shows sheep interacting with two toys as they are being built by a player using the avatar Illykai Pussycat. The left-most toy is a colour changing screen while the right most toy is a shape changing wall. Figure 9.7(b) shows a behavioural cycle developed by one sheep in response to the colour changing toy while Fig. 9.7(c) shows a behavioural cycle developed by a sheep in response to the shape changing wall. Even though the scene includes two toys, when a task becomes highly motivating, sheep are able to focus their attention only on the relevant toy.

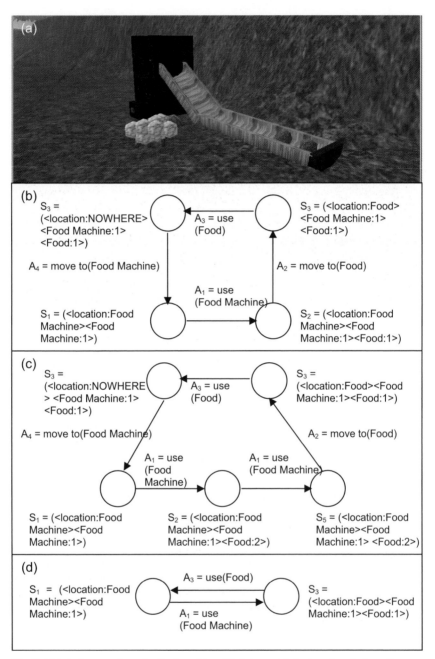

Fig. 9.6 **(a)** A sheep explores the food machine. **(b)** A learned behavioural cycle for eating one food ball at a time. **(c)** A learned behavioural cycle for eating two food balls at a time. **(d)** A learned behavioural cycle for obtaining and eating food without moving.

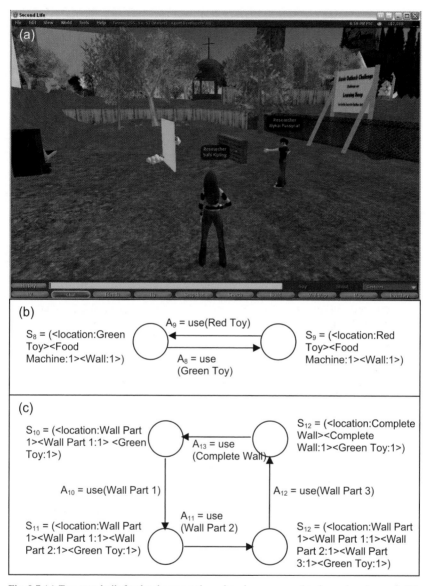

Fig. 9.7 (a) Two toys built for the sheep: a colour changing screen and a shape changing wall. **(b)** A learned behavioural cycle for using the colour changing screen. **(c)** A learned behavioural cycle for using the shape changing wall.

Another of the challenges designed for the sheep was the hoop and target shown in Fig. 9.8. The target was designed with a 'bump detector' that changed its name to 'jump detected' and vice versa each time it was bumped by a sheep. Sheep learned behavioural cycles for walking to the start line and jumping through the hoop. However, behavioural cycles for jumping through the hoop tended to be repeated fewer times than for other tasks, three to four times in comparison to between ten and twenty times or more for other tasks. The reason for this is that the bump detector tended to respond unpredictably due to the *Second Life* physics engine registering multiple bumps during a single collision. While the experiments in Chap. 7 showed that MRL agents can learn in the presence of stochasticity, when the environment is too unpredictable, learning becomes more difficult. This is compounded in motivated reinforcement learning approaches that incorporate interest as a motivation as unpredictable tasks tend to ignored.

Players can also interact with the sheep as they learn. One sheep continued to learn as a player using the avatar Dalrae Herzbrun rode on its back, although the player did not ride for long enough for new behavioural cycles to be learned. In general, while the sheep tended to respond quickly to change in their environment by exploring the results of those modifications, more time was required for repeatable behavioural cycles to be established. This is a property of reinforcement learning in general, that many repetitions of trial-and-error are required for learning to occur.

Aussie Outback Challenge was available for a period of approximately four months. The sheep were switched on for advertised and non-advertised intervals of between three and thirty-six hours over the four-month period. During these four months, *Second Life* citizens designed challenges specifically for the sheep, but also used the land for their own purposes, such as a parking space for vehicles. In both cases, the sheep explored and interacted with designed artefacts.

One of the challenges designed specifically for the sheep was a food area designed by a player represented by an avatar called Ning Nino, shown in Fig. 9.9. This particular challenge proved highly motivating to the sheep while it was being built but less motivating afterwards. While the challenge was being built, Ning Nino made many changes to the environment adding and removing food and creating different types of food including grass, noodles and beef. These changes caused many different but similar events, triggering high interest values.

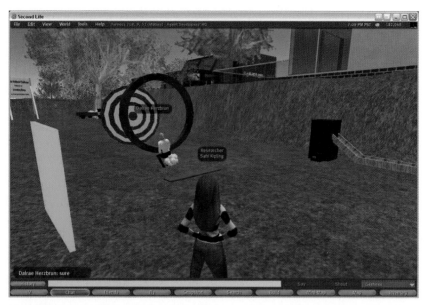

Fig. 9.8. A hoop and target challenge designed for the sheep. A player attempts to ride a sheep while the sheep is learning.

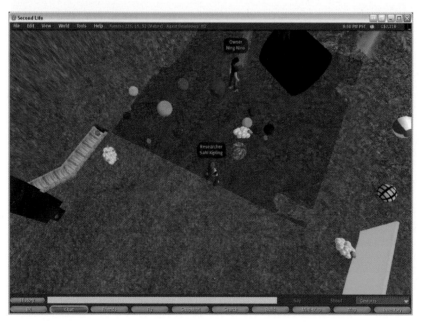

Fig. 9.9 A food pen, with different types of food including noodles, beef and grass.

Another way in which the environment could be modified in *Aussie Outback Challenge* was through the modification of the terrain by creating hills or depressions. One challenge built for the sheep was a hill with a number of stepping stones leading to the top as shown in Fig. 9.10. Sheep learned behavioural cycles for moving from stone to stone to reach the top of the hill and also for jumping directly from the bottom of the hill to the topmost stone.

Two other challenges built for the sheep were a pyramid and a small maze shown in Fig. 9.11. The sheep were able to jump to the top of the pyramid, but due to the small landing platform, they tended to tumble off again in some direction. Because they tumbled in different directions each time, they tended to experience different events each time. This made it difficult to learn to jump to the top of the pyramid as RL requires many identical learning episodes for learning to occur. While some stochasticity can be tolerated the random tumbling proved too unpredictable.

The maze also proved to be somewhat unmotivating for the sheep as all the walls were similarly named "Object" so the sheep did not experience any events as they moved into the maze. The maze may have been more effective if there had been interesting objects inside for the sheep to discover, thus triggering unique events as potential learning tasks.

Fig. 9.10 A hill with stepping stones leading to the top.

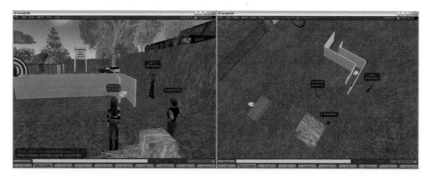

Fig. 9.11 A pyramid and simple maze.

Another challenge built on the playing area by a player using the avatar Dan Medici was a button for creating nuclear missiles, shown in Fig. 9.12. If other players press the button, an arsenal of nuclear weapons results. In this instance, however, the button was not designed to work when sheep attempted to use it. This challenge raises an interesting issue. The primary learning component of MRL is learning by trial-and-error. In dangerous situations or situations where trial-and-error is likely to be obstructive, agents that learn by trial-and-error are undesirable. This suggests that MRL is not currently an attractive solution for implementing the behaviour of NPCs that can suffer permanent death. However, alternative models that combine MRL with social motivation, may be appropriate. This would permit NPCs to learn from the mistakes of other NPCs, or even player characters.

Fig. 9.12 Nuclear missiles built for the sheep.

Fig. 9.13 Response of a sheep to a Terra Airship parked in its paddock, "Sheep 6 whispers: I'm trying to use the Terra Airship 4.0".

Fig. 9.14 The *Aussie Outback Challenge* playing area after four months.

One object not built specifically for the sheep was an airship parked in the game area. Figure 9.13 depicts a sheep attempting to use the Terra Airship. This example illustrates the creative artefacts that can be produced by players in an open-ended virtual world, and the exploratory behaviour of characters controlled by MRL agents.

Figure 9.14 shows the *Aussie Outback Challenge* playing area at the end of the four month experimental period. A range of different challenges are present. The winning challenges that most consistently attract the attention of the sheep are those that incorporate some sort of scripted behaviour. This included the target (which incorporated a scripted 'bump detector'), the colour changing screen and the food machine. This result suggests that the interest function motivates attention focus on dynamic elements of the environment. Intuitively, these elements are interesting because they have behaviours that are unusual when compared to the other static challenges. Anecdotally, this result is pleasing as it parallels the type of attention focus that may be expected from a natural organism.

9.2.1   Discussion

The ability of NPCs using MRL to learn behaviours that adapt to new objects and avatars in their environment makes possible a new generation of games in which players can make open-ended modifications to the game environment while the game is in progress. In *Aussie Outback Challenge*, sheep using MFRL with CFGs are able to respond to modifications to their environment even though the exact changes made by players, or the times and places they will be made, are not known in advance. The behavioural responses of each sheep are based on their experiences in their environment. Because the experiences of each sheep are different, their responses to similar situations can vary, creating a cast of different characters.

While the demonstration in the previous section gives a good indication of the adaptability of MRL agents controlling NPCs, a number of constraints imposed by the *Second Life* virtual environment do limit this demonstration. The speed of the simulation is an issue, with a three second server side delay on XML-RPC calls slowing the simulation considerably. In some cases 24 hours were required before significant behavioural variety was achieved by an individual sheep. A limit of 256 characters per message sent between the client application and the *Second Life* server also limits the number of properties of each object that can be sensed. The CFG representation is flexible enough to allow different objects to be defined in terms of different properties, however this demonstration was limited to sending only the name of sensed objects between the client and server.

Accuracy issues with the *Second Life* physics engine also made it difficult to keep the sheep in their paddock. While the paddock was fenced, sheep that bumped against the fence would continue moving through the fence in some cases. Security restrictions in *Second Life* prevent the sheep from functioning once off their own land, resulting in sheep death. This issue was overcome by allowing dead sheep to re-spawn however any previous learning was lost when the sheep died. Despite these limitations, which it is envisaged will disappear with the continuing improvement in virtual world technologies, the *Aussie Outback Challenge* demonstrates the key concepts of a new kind of open-ended computer game. Players not only have a set of open-ended modelling tools with which they can modify the game environment, but characters are able to reason about and respond to these changes.

9.3 Summary

The development of characters that can respond autonomously to the unpredictable, open-ended changes to their environment is a key challenge in the development of games that allow player characters to make open-ended modifications to the game environment. This chapter has illustrated that MRL provides an approach to this problem. MRL agents permit the development of a new type of NPC that is able to respond to these open-ended modifications. The CFG representation allows the agent to represent the unpredictable, evolving world for character reasoning, without requiring predefined knowledge of the tasks to be learned or human supervision to direct learning. The motivation function provides a way for the NPC to continually identify new learning goals.

In future, open-ended modelling may become an integral part, not just of simulation games, but also role playing games, adventure games and others. For example, the current tools for building houses in massively multiplayer online role-playing games such as *Ultima Online* could be extended to permit open-ended design. With this kind of expansion of existing game genres, a number of questions do arise. For example, players must be able to find key characters such as quest-givers or merchants. This becomes more difficult if characters can move around and explore their environment. As the gap narrows between the adaptability of NPCs and player characters it may become necessary to apply search strategies usually reserved for player characters to NPCs as well.

MRL agents also have higher processing and memory requirements than simple reflex agents. As a result, more resources are required to support similar quantities of characters controlled by MRL agents. However, as the networking and processing capacity of computer technology continues to improve, MRL will offer an appealing alternative to reflex agents for supporting more complex virtual world applications.

9.4 References

[1] Linden, Second Life, www.secondlife.com (Accessed January, 2007).

[2] There.com, www.there.com (Accessed July, 2008).

[3] K. Merrick and M.L. Maher, Motivated reinforcement learning for adaptive characters in open-ended simulation games, ACM SIGCHI International Conference on Advances in Computer Entertainment Technology, (ACE 2007), ACM, Salzburg, Austria, pp. 127–134, 2007.

Part IV
Future

Chapter 10
Towards the Future

Games in multiuser virtual worlds are rapidly introducing new demands on artificial intelligence technologies. As the 3D graphics technology improves the visual quality of non-player characters, there is an expectation that the quality of their behavioural intelligence will also improve. Likewise, because virtual worlds are shared between human-controlled characters and computer-controlled characters, the comparisons between the two will be more common. The task of building believable characters is becoming more and more challenging as the technology around them changes.

This book has presented an in-depth study of a new artificial intelligence technique – motivated reinforcement learning – for application to the design of non-player characters in multiuser games. Motivated reinforcement learning represents a new step forward in the design of non-player characters that can adapt and evolve in time with their changing environment. This in turn opens the way for new types of games in dynamic, multiuser virtual worlds. This chapter looks back at the models and demonstrations presented so far, and reflects on the way they might be used and developed in the future.

10.1 Using Motivated Reinforcement Learning in Non-Player Characters

This book has studied the emergent behaviour of non-player characters (NPCs) controlled by motivated reinforcement learning (MRL) agents in a range of different game scenarios. While these studies provide insight into types of behaviour and environments for which MRL may be appropriate, there is still further work to be done to understand how the approaches described in this book might scale up to even more complex environments. In particular, Chap. 7 did not consider environments made dynamic by the presence of multiple characters. Chapter 8 also explicitly avoided the multiagent scenario by

K.E. Merrick, M.L. Maher, *Motivated Reinforcement Learning*, DOI 10.1007/978-3-540-89187-1_10,
© Springer-Verlag Berlin Heidelberg 2009

designing the sheep such that they cannot sense other sheep. In general, as MRL research progresses, new types of environments and new applications will need to be considered.

At a lower level, a key issue identified by the demonstrations in Chaps. 7 and 8 is the difference in performance between MRL models with and without recall. In general, MFRL models (no recall) displayed significantly faster increases in behavioural variety and complexity than motivated multioption reinforcement learning (MMORL) and motivated hierarchical reinforcement learning (MHRL) models (with recall). However, traditionally, multioption reinforcement learning (MORL) and hierarchical reinforcement learning (HRL) approaches to reinforcement learning (RL) in settings without motivation perform as well as or better than flat RL approaches. These results suggest that there is more work to be done on developing MRL models for the design of NPCs that can recall learned behaviour.

A second key issue with the MRL techniques explored in this book is that, while the motivation models incorporate task selection components that generalise over long experience trajectories, the RL components maintain a state-action table that explicitly maps each state encountered to an action to perform. Use of a state-action table may become infeasible in highly complex environments where the memory requirements to store the table become large. Some existing work in the design computing domain has used MRL with neural network function approximation as an approach to intelligent room applications with very large state spaces [1]. However, a thorough investigation of the impact of function approximation at the learning level on the emergence of task-oriented learning has not been performed.

10.2 Other Gaming Applications for Motivated Reinforcement Learning

Another key focus of this book has been on using MRL to generate character behaviour that can support the plot of a game. However, other applications of MRL in games are also possible. Two examples are the use of dynamic characters to support dynamic difficulty adjustment and procedural content generation.

10.2.1 Dynamic Difficulty Adjustment

Dynamic difficulty adjustment (DDA) [2] is a form of generative level design that takes into account rules about player skills and performance to adapt the game environment while the game is being played. DDA focuses on maintaining players in their flow zone – where the game is most interesting for them – by adapting the challenge level of the game as players develop their skills. Because MRL agents adapt their behaviour in response to their experiences in their environment, there is also potential for them to adapt to player skill level. Such agents might include attributes of player performance in their state representation, permitting them to adapt their behaviour as the values of these attributes change.

10.2.2 Procedural Content Generation

The adaptability of MRL also makes it relevant to structural flow, this time as an approach to procedural content generation (PCG). PCG is the programmatic generation of game content while a game is being played [3]. This may include the layout of characters, objects, terrain and virtual architecture [4].

Previously, techniques for procedural content generation in games have tended to use random and pseudo-random processes to generate an infinite variation of game environments. The main issue with this approach is that it is difficult to distinguish 'good' and 'bad' game environments when they are generated [3]. MRL offers an agent-based approach to PCG in which agents can reason about properties of the existing game environment as a basis for instigating change.

10.3 Beyond Curiosity

The practical sections of this book have focused primarily on cognitively inspired computational models of motivation, including curiosity and competence motivation. However, psychological theory identifies that other models based on biological, cognitive and social motivation are also possible.

10.3.1 Biological Models of Motivation

Computational models based on biological motivation theories may provide a new approach to implementing the behaviour of animals and monsters. The use of motivation in conjunction with flocking algorithms, for example, provides a way to integrate life-like goal-oriented behaviour with traditional flocking [5]. Biological motivation theories may also be relevant to the design of predator–prey relationships between different groups of NPCs or between NPCs and player characters.

10.3.2 Cognitive Models of Motivation

Alternative cognitive models of motivation, such as achievement motivation, also have potential application in MRL to focus attention on different types of tasks. Where interest-based models focus on tasks of moderate novelty, achievement motivation focuses on tasks of either moderate, high or low difficulty, depending on the tendency either to approach success or to avoid failure. Concepts such as achievement motivation have the potential to contribute to a sense of personality in artificial agents and to the identification of critical tasks. The ideas behind achievement motivation could also be useful for managing the structure of the option hierarchy in motivated hierarchical learning models to improve the behavioural variety and complexity of these models.

10.3.3 Social Models of Motivation

Social motivation theories are an important future research direction for MRL in multiagent settings. Evolutionary theories, in particular, represent an important component of motivation models for artificial systems such as reinforcement learning agents designed to function in dangerous environments. They allow adaptation to occur over generations of individuals so that the failure or destruction of a single individual can be tolerated and even used as a trigger for learning within the society as a whole. This sort of adaptation would be particularly useful for the design of enemies or opponents that can learn new ways to combat changing human player tactics.

10.3.4 Combined Models of Motivation

Combined motivation theories are perhaps the ultimate goal towards which computational models of motivation can aspire: comprehensive algorithms that focus attention on biologically, cognitively and socially inspired behaviour. Maslow's hierarchy of needs [6], for example, has parallels in Brooke's subsumption architecture [7] for the design of 'complete creatures'. In Brooks' model, libraries of simple behaviours are subsumed by more complex ones. In MRL, a layered motivational hierarchy has the potential to provide a means of triggering subsumption within a behavioural hierarchy. Such a model would extend Brooks' work with the ability to adaptively generate behaviours at each level of the subsumption hierarchy.

10.4 New Models of Motivated Learning

While MRL was an appropriate choice for the control of certain types of NPCs in gaming environments, in other gaming applications learning by trial-and-error may be inappropriate. For example, trial-and-error would be an inefficient approach to behavioural cloning by partner characters. This does, however, suggest a new branch for the development of motivated learning agents for games, by combining a motivation component with different types of learning components.

10.4.1 Motivated Supervised Learning

The combination of motivation and supervised learning suggests a model for NPCs that can observe the behaviour of player characters and select interesting aspects of that behaviour to mimic. This has applications both to traditional mobile characters such as animals, humanoids or monsters, and also to the design of intelligent gaming environments.

The idea of an intelligent environment has been discussed for physical world buildings that can support and enhance human interaction [8]. However, the idea also has application in games where the environment itself can become the primary antagonist, rather than NPCs in the environment. This idea has been explored in movies such as *Cube* (1997) where rooms can move and contain traps to catch the unwary. The recent *Harry Potter* (2001–) books and movies also play on this idea, with staircases in Hogwarts castle conspiring to confuse students by changing position.

Task-oriented learning using traditional supervised learning algorithms becomes difficult in such environments as the examples available are not filtered to represent individual tasks. In such cases, there is a potential role to be played by motivation to filter examples and focus attention in the learning process. The resulting motivated supervised learning (MSL) algorithms will identify interesting events, and also identify which observations and examples should be allowed through the motivation filter to facilitate learning from those events. Some recent work has explored the idea of intelligent virtual environments using MSL [9].

Unlike RL for which various hierarchical abstraction techniques have been developed to represent high level tasks, similar techniques are uncommon for supervised learning. As with MRL, however, a multitask learning framework for MSL may be useful in certain applications to prevent forgetting learned tasks while attention is focused on other new tasks.

10.4.2 Motivated Unsupervised Learning

Motivated unsupervised learning (MUL) also has potential for developing intelligent gaming environments, taking a similar approach to that described for MSL but allowing the use of unsupervised learning techniques or data mining. Maher et al. [10] have presented models for MSL and MUL agents but as yet no applications of MUL agents exist.

10.5   Evaluating the Behaviour of Motivated Learning Agents

The metrics presented in Chap. 4 of this book measure the performance of MRL approaches in terms of emergent behavioural variety and behavioural complexity. These metrics are designed to evaluate the adaptable, multitask learning ability of MRL approaches without making domain-specific judgements about the algorithm. However, in many applications there is a notion of 'good' and 'bad' behaviour, 'rational' and 'irrational' behaviour or 'intelligent' and 'unintelligent' behaviour – even though it may be difficult to express this behaviour explicitly using rule-based approaches prior to interaction with the environment. Metrics such as the Turing test have been proposed as an approach for distinguishing 'intelligent' behaviour. However other metrics and indeed motivation functions may be required to identify 'good', 'rational' or 'useful' behaviour in specific gaming applications.

10.6 Concluding Remarks

This book is a first step towards building and understanding artificial agents that can learn in complex, dynamic virtual worlds by focusing their attention autonomously based on their experiences in their environment. It has been shown that MRL agents can achieve task-oriented learning using computational models of motivation based on an NPC's experiences in its environment. The models and metrics presented in this book provide a foundation for developing new motivated systems that can respond to their unique experiences in their environment to exhibit rhythmic behavioural cycles for lifelong learning.

10.7 References

[1] O. Macindoe, M.L. Maher and K. Merrick, Agent Based Intrinsically Motivated Intelligent Environments, Handbook on Mobile and Ubiquitous Computing: Innovations and Perspectives, American Scientific Publishers, 2008 (to appear).

[2] J. Chen, Flow in games. http://www.jenovachen.com/flowingames/about.htm, (Accessed July, 2008)

[3] A. Doull, The death of the level designer: procedural content generation in games. http://roguelikedeveloper.blogspot.com/2008/01/death-of-level-designer-procedural.html (Accessed July, 2008).

[4] N. Gu and M.L. Maher, A grammar for the dynamic design of virtual architecture using rational agents. International Journal of Architectural Computing 4(1):489–501, 2004.

[5] R. Saunders and J.S. Gero, Curious agents and situated design evaluations. In: J.S. Gero and F.M.T. Brazier (Eds.), Agents in Design, Key Centre of Design Computing and Cognition, University of Sydney, pp. 133–149, 2002.

[6] A. Maslow, Motivation and personality, Harper, New York, 1954.

[7] R.A. Brooks, How to build complete creatures rather than isolated cognitive simulators. In: K. VanLehn (Ed.), Architectures for Intelligence, Lawrence Erlbaum Associates, NJ, pp. 225–239, 1991.

[8] R.A. Brooks, M. Coen, D. Dang, J. DeBonet, J. Kramer, T. Lozano-Perez, J. Mellor, P. Pook, C. Stauffer, L. Stein, M. Torrance and M. Wessler, The intelligent room project, The Second International Cognitive Technology Conference (CT97), Aizu, pp. 271–279, 1997.

[9] K. Merrick, M.L. Maher and R. Saunders, Achieving adaptable behaviour in intelligent rooms using curious supervised learning agents, CAADRIA 2008, Beyond Computer Aided Design, Chiang Mai, Thailand, pp. 185–192, 2008.

[10] M.L. Maher, K. Merrick and O. Macindoe, Intrinsically motivated intelligent sensed environments, EGICE 2006, Springer-Verlag, pp. 455–475, 2006.

Index